SELF-ESTEEM:
The Necessary Ingredient for SUCCESS

by

SANDI REDENBACH

Edited
by
Carol Souza Cole
Cover design and illustrations
by
Charlie Chung Ho

ESTEEM SEMINAR PROGRAMS/PUBLICATIONS
313 Del Oro Avenue
Davis, CA 95616
(916)756-8678 or (916) 666-0264

Self-Esteem: The Necessary Ingredient For Success
printed in the United States of America
copyright © January, 1991 by Sandi Redenbach

ISBN 0-9632112-0-X (paperback)
Library of Congress
Catalog Card Number 91-090017

Other copywritten publications:
Self-Esteem Awareness Program
A Component of the California Teachers Association High Risk Training Program
Trainer's Manual and Participant's Handbook © 1991
TXU 452-849
ISBN 0-0632112-1-8 Library of Congress
Catalog Card Number 91-090017

All inquiries for materials, permission, workshop presentations, mailing list, etc. can be addressed to:

ESTEEM SEMINAR PROGRAMS and **PUBLICATIONS**
313 Del Oro Avenue
Davis, California 95616
(916) 756-8678

This book is dedicated to all those teachers who empower themselves to make a difference!

Through your efforts, modeling, and committment, the children, - our hope for tommorrow,- will envision and create a future world filled with unconditional love, respect, and full self-expression for everyone.

TABLE OF CONTENTS

"...and the day came when the risk to remain closed in a bud became more painful than the risk it took to blossom!"

Anon.

Branches

Aristotle has been known to proclaim that "the unexamined life is not worth living." It is as if he states that to the degree that we do not reflect upon and evaluate the daily events, circumstances, and purpose of our everyday activity, we are in effect in a state of "waking sleep". He seems to imply that we have at hand the total capacity to nurture and heal ourselves, family, community, nation, and world-completely.

It is possible that by making this type of statement Aristotle is attempting to provoke a response from us. The type of response he is provoking might be phrased in terms of <u>commitment</u>. "Commitment" is a word that seems to have a wide variety of connotations, such as dedication, altruism, giving of oneself, responsibility to one's duty, etc. Sometimes the word "commitment" can be used to imply guilt or shame as if a person is not 100% "committed".

Commitment can also be considered from another point of view, namely that in fact we all are already 100% committed to whatever we "perceive" is in our own best interest at the present time - even though one second later we may realize that the plan or action to which we had been committed was not in our best interest, and we wonder how we could have been so foolish. It may be as in the movie "On

i

Golden Pond" when Katherine Hepburn told Jane
Fonda not to be so hard on her 80 year old father,
Norman (Henry Fonda), "Don't be so hard on
Norman. He is just trying to `make his way.' '"
    Basically we are all trying to "make our way" -
to do the best we can under the confusing conditions,
pressures, standards, and values of modern society.
Thus the question could be phrased not as "Am I a
committed person?" because in fact I am 100%
committed all of the time to what I "perceive" is best at
the time. Rather we can look more at the "quality of
my commitment". Is my response to life all that I am
capable of in my own best interest and in the best
interest of others? Am I and the others with whom I
relate getting all of the payoff we need and deserve
in terms of our physical, mental, emotional, and
spiritual capabilities? Am I really getting the full *bang
for the buck,* getting the full payoff out of life for all
that I put into it everyday?
    In reflecting on the above considerations, the
question of all the dilemmas and contradictions of
modern life becomes glaringly apparent. How can I
take care of myself as well as others at the same
time? I have all I can do just to keep myself together.
What about when I am tired, stressed, overly anxious
or afraid and some one else due to his/her needs
makes some demand on me or expresses a need
that I am expected to fulfill? We all know from daily
experiences how often this happens in terms of
family, employment, and various other relationships.
It often seems like an inherent contradiction or
dilemma because either way they or I don't get what
we (legitimately) need. As Thoreau states: "Most
people lead lives of quiet desperation." There we
are and there we remain...
    Addressing the "quality of commitment"
however provides an exciting alternative. To avoid

wallowing in the state of "waking sleep" implied by Aristotle's statement, we need to recognize that all of the capability to respond to the above scenarios lies within us. We do have the ability and power to resolve these apparent dilemmas and conflicting demands we face daily. The problem is that we are not fully in touch with this power and inner strength. Since we are not in touch or in contact with this inner power, strength, and capability, we do not utilize them in our daily interactions, and consequently life goes on as if we did not possess them.

The challenge here is how to " tap" our inner, latent strengths and potential, bring them to the surface where they can exist consciously and turn into an outward manifestation where they effectively enhance the quality and results of our daily endeavors. The admonition of "Know Thyself !" seems especially pertinent here. The journey of "inward bound" is at least as challenging, fascinating, and perhaps even as terrifying as anything we do in an outer sphere. We need to enhance our thinking, feeling, and reflective processes, to develop an habitual practice of being wholesomely and constructively critical of ourselves without falling into patterns of guilt or self-blame. Insights which we can develop through this process need further work, as a weight lifter must work so many reps if he wants stronger biceps. The insight comes from many different sources and needs to be re-examined and integrated with one another.

Each person or event in life which we encounter can be perceived as coming from its own source or roots much like a tree standing in an orchard among many other trees. Each insight or moment of achieving deeper awareness can be considered as a branch extending from the tree - part of the tree but not all of it. If we pick fruit from a particular branch, it doesn't necessarily mean that we are buying the whole tree. If we consider an idea proposed by someone else and through reflection integrate that idea into our overall value system, it doesn't mean we are buying or approving of everything for which that person stands

Jock Ewing of the TV program "Dallas" once stated that "Power is not something someone gives you; it is something you take." While old Jock undoubtedly was talking about economic and political power, an inference can be applied to personal power: It's a matter of how to "experience yourself powerfully" as opposed to getting caught in "power-plays". It is within my capability to accomplish this. I cannot wait for someone else to come and give it to me. Charisma can be learned and developed; it may be something a person is born with, but not necessarily so. We should feel encouraged to consider but also to be selective about what we accept from others, and to realize that in a very real sense everyone has part of the truth. An exciting endeavor might be to challenge yourself to find that golden thread of truth in everyone you encounter, no matter how offensive or repulsive that person at first might seem. Believe it or not, it's there!

The process of developing deeper understanding of ourselves, others, and the world we live in, can be accomplished realistically by integrating (tying together) each idea and experience (branch) we receive from another person or an event (tree), such that we incorporate into our lives the very best that exists throughout history. If something we realize after reflection doesn't work for us, we simply discard it and move on to utilize what does work for us in accomplishing 100% of our true life purpose.

If a person is to undertake a journey of living a life of such high quality commitment, there are bound to be moments of fear and uncertainty. We should realize that this type of focus on life is a stretch beyond what everyday society can tolerate or approve . It demands an integrity far beyond what is customary. The call for mediocrity has many proclaimers who will campaign for it at all cost; often in very subtle, respectable, and popular ways. We should notice when we are stretching beyond our comfort zone, and how it feels "up there". Take time to stop and "notice", to get your bearings before you move on. Reflection and quiet time are crucial to a serious intention of developing a committed life of high quality, of remaining grounded in your chosen values, and of living out an effective manifestation of these values in modern society.

Make a plan and follow through on it, e.g.,to walk a mile in silence at sunrise for thirty consecutive days, and your life will never be the same. Then utilize your renewed sense of purpose, your increased energy, inner peace, and overall sense of well-being to step out into the world to <u>cause</u> effective change. Utilize all your power, talent, insight, love and energy to witness and manifest the values you hold dearest, and count as your richest satisfaction in life the moments you see others benefit and improve their lives due to your efforts.

----- Jim Korbel

TO THE READER

Self-Esteem: The Necessary Ingredient for Success, came about through numerous requests from teachers who have attended my workshops over the years. They wanted "hard copy" of what I shared in the workshop setting. I have been a teacher for twenty years. For the past eight years, I have provided self-esteem staff development workshops throughout the United States and Canada.along with my full time teaching duties. I began seriously addressing the needs of "at-risk" students through a National Foundation for the Improvement of Education. (NFIE) grant proposal that I wrote six years ago along with two Woodland Joint Unified School District colleagues, Carol Murphey and Pat Blevins Turner. Ours was one of eight grants funded in the nation! (That happening certainly raised my self-esteem.)! While I served as Project Director of the K-12 drop-out prevention grant, the next two years were dedicated to much research and activities with designated "at-risk" students. I also act in a consultant capacity to other teachers and districts who are interested in meeting the needs of "at-risk" students and who are themselves applying for grants. I learned much about what was needed to promote student success, both in the comprehensive traditional school setting, as well as in the arena of alternative education. The experience of coordinating a **drop-out recovery independent study high school program** has added to my convictions that "all students **can** learn and all students **want to** learn." This program, the Independent Learning Center, with its exemplary and dedicated staff, uses self-esteem building techniques as the cornerstone of the curriculum, and has been a major catalyst to the success of many students, who otherwise would not have finished high school, let alone become college success stories.

This teaching experience has been the most rewarding experience of my career. Working with teachers and support staff who are unconditionally loving and supportive, is gratifying beyond words, for our students, as well as for me. There is no way I can thank them enough for their commitment.

The overwhelming reception teachers have given to my workshop messages has been not only encouraging but a tremendous personal learning experience. I have seen firsthand the extraordinary dedication and commitment that my educational colleagues throughout California and the nation exhibit on a day to day basis. Working much of the time against odds that are difficult, trying, and challenging, they persevere. There is no doubt that the general public has little, if any, understanding of what actually goes on, day to day, within the overcrowded, understaffed, monetarily deficient walls of the "average" public school.

The public schools in America are the last bastion of egalitarianism, taking into its fold all children, regardless of physical condition, mental condition, emotional condition, ethnicity, life style, socio-economic status, language barriers, religious conviction, sexual preference, and many other factors which, in some countries, could create a cause for exclusion. Teachers, counselors, nurses, psychologists, support personnel and administrators dedicate their lives to serving America's children, thereby serving and preserving America's past, present, and future.

This book is the culmination of one of my life dreams, the same dream many people have of some day writing their version of "the great American novel". Although this is not a novel, nor is it the final word on the subject of self-esteem, it is my contribution, in print, to teachers and parents. It reflects the teachings of many fine and esteeming people who have studied, worked and taught for years and from who's great wisdom I have profited. The most special of all was the very wonderful Virginia Satir,.author, lecturer, and member of the California State Task Force to Promote Self-Esteem and Personal and Social Responsibility. All who knew Virginia mourn her loss.

I agree with my friend Dianna, who said, "Writing a book is like delivering a baby. You never know how it will turn out."

I want to thank some very special people who helped it to "turn out". Without their support, hard work, and unconditional love, my life would be far less rich and productive:

To **Lance Davis, Carol Souza Cole, and Dennis Scheirmeyer**, three genuinely respected educators, and my esteemed teaching colleagues. You are true friends, who are always there for me, and for the students, day after day. I love you .

To **Dr. Bob Watt**, the best Superintendent in the world, who empowers me daily by trusting me to create and craft my job autonomously, and who acknowledges that I perform it with zest, if not always with patience. I will feel lost without you .

To **Vicki Thoma**, my wonderful, reliable, solid gold secretary, who does a great job, supports my efforts and involvements, smiles even in the face of each new project, wastes no time, and never complains.

To **Amee Fatta**, a beginning teacher who willingly and ably assists at our school to the delight of her students and colleagues. You taught me the meaning of unselfish commitment.

To **BethAnne Darby**, my former Shakespeare student who volunteered so much time to do computer work, make suggestions, and just be there for me, with patience and support., at all hours of the day and night.

To **Charlie Chung Ho,** who labored to create the perfect cover design and chapter separations, and gave excellent artistic advice throughout the process. You are a talented designer.

To **Carol Souza Cole,** for your editing expertise your special friendship and the loving attention you pay to every task you undertake.

To **Esther Wright**, author of <u>Good Morning Class, I Love You,</u> outstanding speaker, and all around wonderful communicator. You are a role model. whose support and friendship are highly valued.

To all of my professional **teacher colleagues** throughout the United States who encouraged me to write and publish this book. Thank you for doing the most important job on earth! And for being willing to do it even better. **You "touch the future".**

And most especially, to my wonderful husband, **Ken Gelatt**, who not only spent time helping, typing, suggesting ideas, and discussing application of concepts, but who has transformed his own teaching in his math classes by using the techniques suggested throughout this book. Thanks for lovingly supporting me through all my traveling and "projects".

If, after reading this book, if any of you have the inclination to discuss public education and how we can collaborate to transform it in this country, or if you want to talk about any ideas in this book, please call or write to me. We are all in this together, and TOGETHER WE MAKE A DIFFERENCE.

With Love and Esteem,

Sandi Redenbach

"In every child who is born, under no matter what circumstances and of no matter what parents, (and of no matter what age,) the potentiality of the human race is born again."
—James Agee

CHAPTER 1

SELF-ESTEEM:

SOME HISTORY, BACKGROUND,
AND RESEARCH

Chapter 1

SELF-ESTEEM:
HISTORY, BACKGROUND AND RESEARCH

Self-Esteem is not a new idea or concept. There have been a great many discussions and studies about how self-esteem affects our lives, our interpersonal relationships, and our successes as members of a society. However, in 1986, the study of self-esteem came into its own through the enactment of California State Assembly Bill 3659, authored by Assemblyman John Vasconcellos, and signed into law by Governor George Deukmejian. The result of the bill was the formation of the **California State Task Force to Promote Self-Esteem and Personal and Social Responsibility.** The purpose of this task force, consisting of 26 members from a variety of backgrounds and walks of life, was to study the effects of self-esteem and its relationship to major social concerns such as family, education and academic failure, drug and alcohol abuse, crime and violence, poverty and chronic welfare dependency, and the work place. Much research has been done, and continues to be done on how healthy self-esteem is nurtured, harmed, reduced and rehabilitated. The final report and publication of that task force, called *Toward a State of Esteem*, addresses all of these areas and gives some key findings and key recommendations for each area.

Although each of these areas and findings impact greatly on the educational system as a whole, including personnel, students, environment, and institutions as well, this book will address itself, as much as possible to what *Toward a State of Esteem* refers to as the area of **Education and Academic Failure**, and how self-esteem impacts upon academic and life successes. Primarily we will concentrate on ways to provide opportunities for academic successes. The intent is to point out ways to build academic success, and high self-esteem for teachers, parents, and students. The basic principles, however, apply to all people in all settings.

Under the area called <u>Recommendations and Discussion</u> in *Toward a State of Esteem* the education and academic failure section states:

> "If the family is the first in importance in nurturing self-esteem, the schools are second. More than in any other single area of our study, schools have demonstrated the centrality of self-esteem. Schools that deliberately nurture self-esteem have recorded impressive results in academics as well as in social and personal responsibility."

The Task Force is recommending that every school district make a conscious effort to promote self-esteem and personal and social responsibility. Because good education requires good self-esteem, the Task Force recommends that training in this area be a part of the teacher credentialing process and a part of all in-service training. Many school districts and individual schools have begun to address these recommendations by providing workshops on self-esteem. Continued training in this area is important.

TOWARD A STATE OF ESTEEM

There are eleven key recommendations in the California State Task Force to Promote Self-Esteem and Personal and Social Responsibility publication *Toward a State of Esteem.* The first two are stated in detail followed by a summary of all eleven.

Key Recommendations on Education and Self-Esteem

1. Every school district in California (and throughout the country-*author's note*) should adopt the promotion of self-esteem and personal and social responsibility as a clearly stated goal, integrate self-esteem in its total curriculum, and inform all persons of its policies and operations.

   School boards should establish policies and procedures that value staff members and students and serve to foster mutual respect, esteem and cooperation.

2. Course work in self-esteem should be required for credentials and as a part of in-service training for all educators.

   At least one course in the nature and development of self-esteem (in one's self and in one's students) should be required for credentials in teaching, counseling, or administration and for maintaining those credentials. School districts should develop and expand training in the development of self-esteem and personal and social responsibility as part of their on-going staff development programs.

Summary of Recommendations

1. Self-esteem and responsibility must be woven into the total educational program.
2. Educate every educator -- through pre-service and in-service training -- in self-esteem and responsibility.
3. Give students opportunities to do community service.
4. Formulate a real-life skills curriculum.
5. Promote more parent involvement.
6. Be sensitive to the needs of students at risk of failure.
7. Use the arts to help develop self-esteem and responsibility.
8. Expand counseling and peer counseling services for students.
9. Provide cooperative learning opportunities.
10. Reduce class size or student and adult ratios.
11. Implement programs to counteract bigotry and prejudice.

Summary of Self-Esteem Research Supporting the Significance of Self-Esteem (compiled by Robert Reasoner)

1. Drop-outs

    * School dropouts tend to have more negative self-esteem as learners than those who stay in school. (Bloom, 1977)

4

* Two common characteristics among girls dropping out of school include low academic achievement and low self-esteem. (Janice Earle, 1987)

* A major factor in school drop-outs is not hostility to the system, but strong feelings of inadequacy and internal blame, feeling they don't have the intelligence or the ability to succeed, in other words, low self-esteem reinforced consciously or unconsciously by parents or teachers. (Hyman Kite,1989)

2. Delinquency, Crime and Violence

* Found a correlation between delinquency and low self-esteem and found evidence of a link between increased self-esteem and a reduction of delinquent behavior. (Kelley, 1978)

* Reports that maintenance of one's self-esteem is a powerful motivation. Violations to self-esteem occur through insult, humiliation, or coercion and this becomes a tremendous source of anger and hostility which frequently results in violence. (Kaplan)

* Found evidence that for individuals with low self-esteem who have experienced consistent failure, delinquent behavior serves to enhance self-esteem as a way of getting back at the system. (Kaplan)

* Found that juvenile delinquency prevention programs often fail because they overlook the crucial element of self-esteem and its impact on reducing delinquent behavior.(Johnson, 1977)

* Study of Vandalism in West Germany. shows this behavior permits powerless individuals to strike out against the institutions which control them and to take charge of the situation themselves, thereby raising their self-esteem.

3.   Alcohol and Drug Abuse

* Low self-esteem either causes or contributes to neurosis, anxiety, defensiveness, and ultimately alcohol and drug abuse. (Andrew Keegan, 1987)

* States that those with a strong sense of self do not have to be sustained at the expense of others. They do not need to control or humiliate other people or resort to substance abuse. (Skager, 1988)

* Results of his study show considerable deficiencies in self-esteem among drug-dependent patients, and believes that teenagers with low self-esteem who are exposed to drugs may be considered to be at-risk. (Gossop, 1976)

4.   Teenage Pregnancy

*   The relationship between pregnancy and self-esteem depends to some degree on whether it is considered deviant behavior. A girl with low self-esteem may be unconcerned about avoiding pregnancy simply because there is little to lose if she becomes pregnant. In other cases, it is expected as a cultural norm and is not considered deviant so there is no impact on self-esteem. (Crockenberg and Soby,1989)

*   The authors did find that in 4 of 5 studies, low self-esteem is associated with less frequent or less sustained use of contraceptives.   (Crockenberg and Soby, 1989)

*   Approximately one million adolescent women become pregnant each year. Eighty-five percent (85%) to ninety-five percent (95%) elect to keep their babies rather than give them up for adoption in the belief that a baby will provide the kind of unconditional love and acceptance that they perceive society does not. (Beane, 1984)

*   The PACE `report on the conditions of children in California reports that twenty-five (25) percent of all the children being born today are being born to single mothers. (Kirst, 1990)

5.   Other Relationships

*   His research   confirms the relationship between depression in adolescents and low self-esteem. (Battle, 1987)

*   An adolescent's self-concept is the single most important factor in determining a child's response to peer pressure. (Hagedorn, 1979)

*   Found a high correlation between moral decision-making and the level of self-esteem. The higher the self-esteem, the less cheating and stealing there was, and the more they were concerned about the common good. (John Whitely, 1980)

*   Reported that those with self-esteem more consistently offered help and behaved more responsibly toward others. (Wilson, 1976)

*   States, "We believe low self-esteem is the underlying   psychological   mechanism underlying   all   deviant   behavior". (Steffenhagen & Burns, 1988)

6.   School Achievement

* Found there was a significant relationship between self-esteem and school achievement. (Brookover, Thomas, and Patterson, 1985)

* Found that children's self-concept predicated a child's ability to read in first grade at least as well as did I.Q. (Coopersmith, 1965)

* There is considerable empirical evidence that self-concept predicates and influences achievement in school, from the primary grades through undergraduate education. (Wylie, 1979)

* Found it becomes important to determine and promote the change-producing variables involved in effective experiences that enhance student self-concept and academic achievement. (Leamon, 1982)

* Academically related self-esteem appears to be an effect rather than a cause of academic achievement. Although high self-esteem can facilitate academic success, it does not in itself cause achievement. (Holly, 1987)

* Self-esteem needs to be firmly grounded in competencies and achievements worthy of esteem. (Holly, 1987)

* Students do fare better both academically and socially if they have a realistic self-image, a sense of personal worth, and a confidence in their own abilities. (Holly, 1987)

A large number of studies over the past 75 years have demonstrated a positive association between self-esteem variables and academic achievement. A review of correlational studies reports a positive association between achievement and as do achievement scores; and as self-esteem decreases, so does achievement. (Covington, 1989)

* The accumulated weight of evidence suggests that all those attributes we have associated with self as a personal resource can be modified through direct instruction and that such instruction can lead to achievement gains. (Covington, 1989)

RESEARCH FINDINGS: HOW TEACHERS IMPACT ON STUDENTS

The following pieces of research are clearly indicative of just how important teachers and the whole process of learning can be in regards to students and self-esteem. Reading some of the research in its complete form is indeed an eye opener and could be required reading for every teacher, especially those who may forget for even one moment how important an influence teachers are in the lives of children..

1.   Students who feel good about themselves and their abilities are the ones most likely to

succeed. Academic success or failure is deeply rooted in self-esteem. (Brookover, Campbell, Bledsoe, Paterson and Thomas)

2. The way to building positive and realistic self-images in students lies largely in what the teacher believes about himself. (Rosenthal and Jacobson)

3. The more positive students' perceptions are of their teacher's feelings, the better the academic achievement and the more desirable their classroom behavior, as rated by the teacher. (Clarke and Brookover)

4. Teachers need to view students in positive ways and hold favorable expectations and student academic success will result. (Combs, Davidson, Lang, and Clarke)

5. Achievers are characterized by self-confidence, self-acceptance, and a positive self-concept. (Gowan and Brunkan)

6. Poor reading ability is closely bound up with feelings of personal worth. (Zimmerman and Allebrand)

7. Self-concept and academic ability is associated at each grade level. (Thomas and Paterson)

8. Underachievers consistently have negative self-concepts. (Goldberg)

9. Underachievers see themselves as less adequate and less accepted by others. (Combs)

10. Underachievers are more withdrawing, lack self-reliance, a sense of personal worth and a feeling of belonging. (Durr and Schmats)

11. Poor performance in school lowers self-regard and successful performance raises self-regard. Success or failure in school significantly influences the ways in which students view themselves. (Carlton and Moore)

12. A child's behavior is a function of the expectation of others who are significant to him. The expectations of significant others are internalized into self-perceptions. (Shaw, Dutton, and Brookover)

13. Parents are critical in molding and maintaining a child's self-image. (Manis)

14. Many children's capacity to love is permanently inhibited because important people fail to provide warmth and affection when it is needed most. (Block)

Knowing this information now, let's turn to what constitutes an **"At-Risk"** environment.

CHAPTER 2

BEING "AT RISK":

AT HOME AND IN SCHOOL

"Feelings of worth can only flourish in an atmosphere where individual differences are appreciated, mistakes are tolerated (celebrated), communication is open, and rules are flexible-the kind of atmosphere that is found in a nurturing family."

—Virginia Satir

Chapter 2

BEING "AT RISK":   AT HOME AND IN SCHOOL

Many of our young people today, feel inadequate, unhappy, and restless. They are at "**AT-RISK**". We are confronted daily with tangible evidence of drug abuse, teen pregnancy, homelessness, alcoholism, and attitudes of giving up because "I can't do anything right anyway". At the very core or nucleus of these major social problems is the over-riding personal problem of **low self-esteem**, which creates and impacts on all the others.

According to Cindy Collins, a mentor teacher in the Ridgecrest School District, in Ridgecrest, California:

Some of the real problems of youth today are:
1. Low Self-Esteem
2. Poor Communication Skills
3. Inadequate Coping Skills
4. Inability to handle conflict and anger constructively
5. Lack of knowledge about alternatives, options, and choices
6. Not understanding the consequences of their behavior
7. Unrealistic expectations about relationships, marriage, family life, and careers
8. Misunderstanding of male/female roles

These same problems are pervasive with an ever growing number of people of all ages throughout our entire population.   This fact is manifest in day to day living as we read the newspapers and witness people victimizing and being victimized. In this book, the focus will be on young people, whom I will call students. They are learning, growing and representing the hope of the future. The information offered, however, is generic to people of all ages, ethnicities, socio-economic levels, and walks of life.   In the past, many of the above mentioned problems were handled in the home. This was at a time when parents or at least mother was at home. The problems throughout society have increased and there are fewer parents at home to take care of things. Presently these problems are creating difficulties for our young people, for parents, for teachers, and for our schools. Even though we would like the family to solve these problems, much of the time this does not seem possible or likely for a variety of reasons. Therefore it becomes critical to develop a partnership with the home, the community and the **schools**, which are truly the **last best hope** for our students' futures, and indeed for our own. In fact, everyone throughout the community and the private business sector must act to help deal with these issues.   The enormous problems of youth are polarizing our country. We must recognize these problems, the myriad social and family dysfunctions, and address them in a collaborative manner.

When teachers and parents attend workshops and trainings on such things as gangs, adolescent suicide, teen pregnancy, child abuse, drop-out prevention, alcohol and drug abuse, among others, they address the **symptoms** that students and adults manifest. At the root of these symptoms lies the cause, **low self-esteem.** We must recognize this cause, and acknowledge the damage it does to individuals, families, the work place, and the society in general. We must then put into practice ways to turn low self-esteem into a more realistic picture of what values and contributions each person has and makes, so that each person can begin to esteem him/herself more highly. I agree that, "Looking at self-esteem as the end product is like pulling up the flower to look at the roots." (Burl Waits)

Self-Esteem Building is a process that works at the source of most of these difficulties. However in order to build self-esteem, students, teachers, parents, and all of society, must acquire the knowledge and skills to develop high self-esteem. This book will present ways in which all people, and especially teachers and parents can acquire this needed knowledge and skill and pass it on to others as well. I have made this book as generic as possible so this information can be used in all arenas of society, the home and family, schools, businesses, and government. We must be ready to embrace a shift in our paradigms and stop looking for cures from the outside. The only valuable "cure" comes from the recognition that each of us is a part of the whole and can bring about, with assistance, our own empowerment. When we do that we have empowered others as well.

Some of the objectives of this book are to provide the reader with an opportunity to:
1. Understand the definition of, the meaning of, and the key elements of self-esteem.
2. Determine the types of communication skills important for the development of self-esteem.

3. Learn ways to model and share these skills in the classroom, in the family, and in business.
4. Develop ways to teach students how to be responsible in important areas of their academic and personal lives.
5. Create opportunities for empowering students, parents, and teachers to take responsibility for events in their lives.

It is apparent that we must do what is necessary to assist young people through the process of maturation and education, to realize how capable they are of learning, of taking responsibility for their actions, and of being in control of their own lives. The findings of the California State Task Force to Promote Self-Esteem and Personal and Social Responsibility has documented just how important a role parents, the schools, and teachers play in building self-esteem.

We can begin to understand the process of how self-esteem is gained and lost for ourselves as we grow in maturity toward adulthood if we know some of the data that has been gathered by many different individuals and scholarly researchers.

For example, according to research done by the Quest Foundation in Columbus, Ohio, students encounter the equivalent of **60 days** each year of **reprimanding, nagging, and punishment.** During 12 years of schooling a student is subjected to 15,000 negative statements per year. That's three times the number of positive statements received. Is it any wonder that students feel they are "bad", "incapable", "losers", etc.?

In an interview of 2000 kids in 120 high schools, Rick Little, founder of the Quest Foundation asked them these two questions:

1. What are the top two problems you have in your life?
2. If you were to develop a program for your high school to help you cope with what you are meeting now in your life, and what you think you will meet in the future, what would the program include?

The most frequent answers to the first question were:

    I. Loneliness (even popular kids felt lonely)
    2. Not liking themselves

The answers to the second question were as follows:

    I. Responsibility
    2. Respect for self and others
    3. Reality
    4. Relationship skills

Where are the simple past days of reading, 'riting, and 'rithmatic? Could these be the **new "four R's"** of education?   Perhaps we must move to seven R's in this time of restructuring schools. It seems that what needs to be taught in both life and school is not so simple anymore.

One other piece of data, the source of which I do not recall, done in 1982, which supports the importance of building self-esteem in our students, asked 160,000 seniors in the U.S., **"As you look ahead to the future, what's the one thing you want most out of life?** The most frequent answer was **"To be loved."** It is my guess that this meant "unconditional love".

The University of Iowa did a study on average two year old children and the messages they receive. There were 432 negative or controlling statements per day as compared to only 32 positive and affirming statements per day. This is a ratio of 13.5 to 1. (Source: Dr. Jack R. Gibb) Is it any wonder that by the time we get them in school they already feel unhappy about who they are?. And when we add the Quest research on nagging and punishment mentioned above, it is no wonder why we have such a high rate of dropouts, suicides, alcohol and drug addiction, gang memberships, etc. Since the following information was gathered in 1985, there is a strong indication that among young people there has been little significant change for the better, and in fact, there is much to support that there are more pressures and negatives in this day and age than ever before as far as young people and adults are concerned. These negatives seem to build and have a greater impact on individuals as they move through the academic years, and they stay with us.

For example the Gallup Organization, in 1985, discovered through their research the following: **80%** of the students **entering kindergarten** or first grade, have high self-esteem, (feel good about themselves) by **fifth grade** it has dropped to **20%** and by the time they are **seniors** in **high school**, the number has dropped to 5%. In fact, <u>two out of three Americans suffer from low self-esteem.</u> It is often a hidden fact because few, if any, people want others to suspect that they may not feel good about who they are. But low self-esteem shows through behavior patterns that people of all ages exhibit. Some of the things to look for are habitual expressions of:

Not feeling cared about
Not feeling a sense of belonging
Not feeling they have control over their own life
Not feeling a sense of power
Not feeling heard
Not feeling they have a say
Not feeling important anywhere

These expressions in conjunction with the following put people in the "at risk" category:

    a lack of internal self-control
    a lack of adequate support systems
    a lack of effective decision-making skills
    a lack of appropriate coping skills
    being reactive to life situations
    exhibiting a "victim" mentality

This is where schools and teachers, properly equipped, can begin to make a difference in the life trend of "at risk" people.

When the National Institute of Education asked one thousand, thirty year old people if they felt that their schooling had equipped them with the "skills they needed for the real world", more than 80% said, "Absolutely not". When asked what skills they wished they had been taught, they said the following:

1. **Relationship skills (how to get along better with the people with whom I am living.)**
2. **How to find and keep a job**
3. **How to handle conflict**
4. **How to be a good parent**
5. **The meaning of life**

Although it may be difficult for most of us to teach "the meaning of life", it is very possible to equip students with other tools; the tools which will encourage them to value themselves, others, and life itself.

We will attack the basic fundamental ways in which teachers and parents can, within their own capabilities, begin to teach and model the things that former students find of great value outside of the school arena,- in that arena called "life".

There are several things to be achieved from reading, understanding, implementing, and practicing the information given in this book. Teachers, parents, and everyone who wishes to transform their inter-personal relationships, gain a level of empowerment, and improve their general happiness as well as experience some degree of personal growth.

FOR TEACHERS:

- o By interacting positively with their students, they will have a major impact on both their own and their student's self-esteem .
- o By fostering the development of self-esteem in their students, they will discover ways to make the classroom safe for students to take academic risks and challenge their own untested abilities.
- o By teaching assertive communication skills, they will model ways for students to gain some control over their ability to communicate.
- o By developing situations where the students can practice being responsible, teachers will raise self-esteem and hence, raise academic achievement.
- o By doing this under the umbrella of curriculum, students will grow academically and socially and become more successful and responsible citizens.

FOR PARENTS:

- o Students will begin to make a deeper commitment to contribution.to the family unit Instead of "taking" from the family in "you owe me" fashion, they will begin to understand the idea of "give and take".

o   Students will achieve a fuller sense of self
and the connection one has to the family
unit, no matter what the structure of that
unit may be.

Self-Esteem and its Relationship to the Educational Process

There has been much controversy about the
role that self-esteem plays or "should" play in the
educational process. Some people are convinced
that self-esteem building techniques consist of a
"bunch of touchy-feely psycho-babble", others want
schools to "stop playing psychiatrist and get down to
the business of book learning". While either of these
perspectives have their place, based upon the
socialization processes of their proponents, there is
ample research and documentation which
substantiates the importance and necessity of
schools addressing the issue of self-esteem. **Self-
esteem has a direct correlation to the issue of
academic achievement.** Although even outside of
the arena of school, self-esteem relates to one's
success at being a member of a family, success on
an interpersonal level, success in the work place,
and success in the community, the development of
self-esteem in the schools is a bit different.

It is imperative that the **entire classroom
experience** be used as a vehicle in which student
self-esteem is strengthened. Those people who
think that schools can be "reformed" and
"restructured" successfully without the assurance that
every student will grow in self-worth so they can
succeed academically during school years, are
unclear about the relationship between learning and
self-worth. It is impossible to continue to "educate"

children in academic subjects in hopes that they will be successful contributing members of their society from simply learning their ABC's. **The whole human being must be educated.** The whole human being carries the burdens of social problems, economic problems, family problems, community problems., and interpersonal relationship problems.

In a recent edition of *Teacher Connections, Office of Teaching Support Newsletter,* California Department of Education, the following thoughts were offered. "...The goal of restructuring is to dramatically improve the conditions for learning and teaching and the achievement outcomes of *all* students. At the heart of restructuring is the belief that all students, regardless of race, ethnic, linguistic, or socioeconomic background, need to learn to think critically, solve problems individually or as part of a team, analyze and interpret new information, develop convincing arguements, and apply their knowledge to new situations. Restructuring requires schools and districts to challenge fundamental assumptions about the purpose of schooling and to transcend traditional bounds of thinking to create a learning environment that engages all students in active, thinking, meaning-centered learning experiences.

Restructuring should be centered around the vision of the school community, in real world terms, of what it is the community wants students to be able to do, know, and be at the end of their school experience. Outcomes expressed in terms of demonstrable skills, knowledge, and attitudes that are desired of students should drive the curriculum, instruction, and organizational structures of the school. This is in marked contrast to the traditional "rulebased" school systems that use hours of "seat time", numbers of programs or services offered, and so forth, as measures of school success". Once again, the whole human being must be educated.

When we go back to the study that was done by the California Task Force to Promote Self-Esteem and Personal and Social Responsibility, looking closely at only two of their key findings we see that "people who esteem themselves are less likely to engage in destructive and self-destructive behaviors", and the school environment plays a major role in the development of self-esteem"; and "schools that feature self-esteem as a clearly stated component of their goals, policies, and practices are more successful academically as well as developing healthy self-esteem."

To have high self-esteem, we must feel intellectually competent, personally responsible, useful to others, and accepted for who we are. There are two places where those things must be attended to and nurtured, **the home and the school.** Keeping that in mind, let's look at what constitutes self-esteem.

CHAPTER 3

WHAT IS SELF-ESTEEM?:

THE NECESSARY INGREDIENT FOR SUCCESS

CHAPTER 3

WHAT IS SELF-ESTEEM?
The Necessary Ingredient for Success

Research has documented the important role high self-esteem plays in academic achievement and social and personal responsibility. For all people of all ages the development of full human potential is enhanced through high self-esteem. High self-esteem can begin to develop when the acceptance of all individuals and their personal and group contributions are recognized and applauded, especially in a multi-culturally diverse world.

Self-esteem is the **one key ingredient** that affects the **level of proficiency** in all fields of endeavor. Self-esteem has been correlated to: job success, school achievement, interpersonal compatibility, and general happiness.

There are many definitions of self-esteem some of which we will explore within these pages. According to Dr. Robert Ball, former Executive Director of the California Task Force to Promote Self-Esteem and Responsibility, "...self-esteem is not, blowing yourself kisses in the mirror every day". It is more all-encompassing and pervasive, dealing with the total human being.

The definition of self-esteem from the California State Task Force to Promote Self-Esteem and Personal and Social Responsibility, taken from the State Task Force Publication, *Toward a State of Self-Esteem* says self-esteem is:

Appreciating my own worth and importance and having the character to be accountable for myself and to act responsibly toward others.

Each part of this definition can be analyzed in more detail as follows:

1. **Appreciating our worth and importance** involves accepting ourselves, setting realistic expectations, forgiving ourselves and others, taking risks, trusting,and expressing feelings. It also rests on appreciating our creativity, our minds, our bodies, and our spiritual beings.

2. **Appreciating the worth and importance of others** means affirming each person's unique worth, giving personal attention, and demonstrating respect, acceptance, and support. This principle also means setting realistic expectations, providing a sensible structure, appreciating the benefits of a multi-cultural society, accepting emotional expressions, and negotiating rather than being abusive.

3. **Affirming accountability for ourselves** requires taking responsibility for our decisions and actions, being a person of integrity, and understanding, affirming our values, attending to our physical health, and taking responsibility for our actions as parents.

4. **Affirming our responsibility toward others** means respecting the dignity of being human, encouraging independence, creating a sense of belonging, developing basic skills, providing physical support and safety, fostering a democratic environment, recognizing the balance between freedom and responsibility, balancing cooperation and competition, and serving humanity.

Another definition of self-esteem often used says:

Self-Esteem is a subjective evaluation of worth. It is a process influenced by feelings of competence and personal effectiveness.

This definition focuses on how much one feels he or she is worth and how capable and effective one sees oneself as being. It is somewhat more personal.

The definition that this author prefers is as follows:

"Self-Esteem is self-confidence, self-worth and self-respect. It involves respecting others, and also feeling a sense of harmony and peace within yourself."

People of any age or lifestyle can certainly relate to this definition. It has the components of an "I can" attitude. It allows for a clearly defined connection to others on the planet and fosters a sense of well being for an individual. The most important part of the definition is the promise of a sense of harmony and peace within yourself

Harmony and peace are the internal feelings that everyone dreams of having.

All these definitions are correct and it doesn't matter which one you use. A sense of self-esteem, self-concept, and self in general increases one's understanding of the world as a whole.

To measure your own level of self-esteem, Ken Blanchard and Jennifer James have developed, for their audio tape series on <u>Inner Management: The Importance of Self-Esteem</u>, the following self-assessment questions:

1. Are you a critical person? Do you find fault with others easily?
2. Do you allow yourself to make mistakes? Are you a perfectionist?
3. Do you like your physical image? Do you think you are attractive?
4. Do you have a good sense of humor? Are you able to see the humor in everyday situations?
5. Do you laugh easily? Are you able to laugh at yourself---your shortcomings or mistakes?
6. Can you say "no" to others' requests for your time? Do you value your time highly?
7. Do you like your name? If not, would you consider changing it?
8. How do you feel about your birthday? Is it a day to celebrate or a day to hide?
9. Are you argumentative? Do you feel a need to be right all the time?
10. Are you intolerant of others? Do you resent people who are significantly different than you?

11. Are you an angry or grouchy person? Do you become angry easily?
12. Are you able to "forgive and forget?" Do you tend to hold a grudge?
13. Are you a jealous person? Do you fear having people or things taken away from you?
14. Are you materialistic? Do you feel the need to display your possessions?
15. Do you request that others only address you by your proper name or title? Do you display your credentials, awards or certificates?
16. Do you have the ability to recover quickly from a loss or failure? Do you find someone else to blame for your failures?

Your answers will allow you the opportunity to evaluate areas in which you would like to grow.

Facts about Self-Esteem

Self-esteem is the one key ingredient that affects the level of proficiency in all fields of endeavor. Self-esteem has been correlated to job success, school achievement, interpersonal compatibility and general happiness. **Low self-esteem** has been cited as the culprit behind such social maladies as **crime, drug and alcohol addiction, school drop-outs, suicide, sexual promiscuity, habitual lying, defensive behavioral patterns.**

The building and improvement of self-esteem can be done when one separates the various elements of how self-esteem is formed. These elements can be addressed both individually and in concert as a total unit. When working to improve physical strength or learning to play a musical instrument one works with each basic element separately as well as with all the elements together. It is the same in building self-esteem. Self-esteem develops when the primary needs of a person's life have been appropriately satisfied. (See Maslow's Hierarchy of Needs on page 36)

High self-esteem can be gained when people experience positive feelings within four distinct conditions or elements. Many people have different ways to describe these elements. Clemes and Bean label them **connectiveness, uniqueness, empowerment, and models**. Michelle Borba calls them **affillation, identity, mission, and competence,** and Bob Reasoner uses **belonging, selfhood, sense of purpose and roles** These are the basic areas in which we can look toward building self-esteem. The names we give these areas are only important **to identify specific behaviors** in order to change or modify them. Let's highlight how each fits into the four elements of self-esteem as Clemes and Bean describes them.

<u>Connectiveness</u> results when a person gains satisfaction from associations that are significant to that person, and the importance of those associations has been affirmed by others.

For example being a member of the school choir or ecology club gives students a sense of connectiveness or belonging. The relationships developed and/or the feeling of prestige gained enhance the student's self-esteem. The same thing is true when teachers make the student's presence in the classroom seem important. Telling a child who has been absent how much you missed him/her promotes that feeling of connectiveness. Any deliberate action that shows or tells a person how valuable they are to have as a part of a group, family, organization, classroom, or activity builds self-esteem. A lack of that type of action can tear a person's self-esteem to shreds.

Connectiveness deals with a person's feeling of acceptance by groups of people s/he considers important. One of the best ways to foster this feeling is to help the student feel accepted at home and in the classroom. Any activity that brings the students together will develop a sense of belonging. Class nicknames, mottos, rituals, etc. all enhance a student's sense of connectiveness. The reason young people join gangs is to increase their sense of belonging. This is the same reason grown men join clubs like the Elks, the Moose, Kiwanis, Lions, and private country clubs.

Everyone wants to feel like they belong. Knowing how important and necessary a part of the human condition it is to be affiliated, gives us insight into why we have so much anger and mistrust toward those who "cast us out" or leave us out. Take the sibling in a family or classroom who is said to be "different" in some way, maybe he/she is said to be less organized than a sister, or not as smart as a brother, not as athletic as another sister. Regardless of whether it is a child in a particular family or a person of a different race, ethnicity, sexual orientation, or religion, the subconscious message is the same, "I do not belong". What we need to be doing is making sure that everyone feels they are valuable and that they do belong. There are some exercises and suggestions later in the book to help determine how to build in a sense of belonging when dealing with children.

Uniqueness **occurs when a person can acknowledge and respect the qualities or attributes that make him/her special and different, and when that person receives respect and approval from others for those qualities.**

For example, knowing and stating that a student can crochet or play racquetball or that they are a good listener helps to enhance their self-esteem by acknowledging strengths upon which they can build. It also allows other students or family members to see that everyone has gifts and talents that are respected, and that not everyone needs to be the same. In a remote way, a sense of uniqueness helps to promote a sense of community. It is ironic that when people are acknowledged for the unique qualities they have, they tap those qualities more often which allows them to get better and better at those qualities. If we were to notice positive qualities about everyone, we could be instrumental in helping people discover more of their personal bests as well as motivating them to make use of their special gifts and talents.

People feel unique or special when they can acknowledge the attributes or abilities that make them special. Having a teacher or parent or significant other also acknowledge a student's selfhood solidifies their sense of identity. Positive and encouraging recognition from a teacher or parent during or after an activity in which students are discovering things about themselves is very crucial to the development of this element of self-esteem. There are many activities that teachers and parents can initiate to help youngsters discover their sense of self.

Empowerment comes about through having the resources, opportunity, and capability to influence the circumstances of ones' own life in important ways. Taking responsibility for keeping track of homework assignments, making a decision about whether to go to a concert with their friends or to take their little brother to the zoo as they promised, are all examples of students gaining a sense of control over their lives. Knowing that they are in control of important parts of their lives and that they are empowered to make choices which impact on their time, comfort, money, and ability, builds their self-esteem.

Many people who feel "powerless" act out through expressions of anger. They seem to experience "control" as something others have over them. They experience control as external rather than internal .The locus of control. must be internal if people are to feel "in control". People feel they have power when they are able to influence situations in their lives in important ways.

Giving students some input into the development of the classroom operating procedures is one way that students can feel they have some control over their academic lives. At home, allowing children to have some say in determining the rules of the household will give them a sense of empowerment as well. The old "when you are under my roof you will do as I say" days are gone. It just does not work anymore, especially if we want to build a sense of empowerment in young people. Teaching assertive communication skills is very important in developing a student's sense of purpose. We will discuss this communication technique shortly.

Models reflect a person's ability to refer to adequate human, philosophical, and operational examples that serve to help him/her establish meaningful values, goals, ideals, and personal standards.

Having someone in their life to model cultural values, to model a willingness to take positive risks and responsibilities, to model assertive communication skills and ways for making positive choices gives students a chance to obtain these skills and attitudes for themselves. Since we have control over only one person, ourselves, it becomes very important that we, as teachers and parents model these skills and attitudes for our students. If we walk around complaining that we are victims of a system or government , the child sees and internalizes that modeling. The same is true for all the positive modeling we exhibit. Because people need to feel competent in some area of their life, recognizing students strengths and emphasizing them rather than dwelling on their weaknesses has such a great effect on their willingness to cooperate, concentrate, and create in the classroom, at home and in the community.

Teachers provide the modeling for student behavior. It is in this arena the we hope to determine how a student comes to view the world and his/her role in it at least as far as knowledge acquisition is concerned. Sometimes parents do not provide good modeling, so at least the child has this opportunity in the classroom to see a wholesome world view and develop his/her own world view from teachers' modeling This is only one of many reasons teachers are so very important in the life of a child. A teacher could clearly be the only ray of hope for a child from a dysfunctional family. Many people tell of having been "saved" by a teacher from a life role seemingly predetermined by the family unit. Through the teacher model, a child can view positive future possibilities.

All four of these conditions should be present continuously for a sense of high self-esteem to be developed and maintained. No one condition is more important than another. If any one condition is not adequately provided for, there is a decrease or distortion of self-esteem. **All of the above must occur in an atmosphere of security. Students need to feel safe and secure both physically and emotionally in order for the other ingredients to be present in great abundance.** This fact becomes increasingly clear as we move to Maslow's Hierarchy of Needs.

MASLOW'S HIERARCHY OF NEEDS

Abraham Maslow was a psychologist who spent a great deal of time studying the human condition. He developed a theory about people and their needs for fulfillment. His research and findings are respected and widely acknowledged. When we look at Maslow's "Hierarchy of Needs" Model we see the levels or steps of a pyramid that shows the **basic** and beyond basic needs of every human being.

Maslow said that it is close to impossible for people to move from one level to another, up the ladder, if the needs on each lower rung are not first fulfilled to some extent. It is not known to what extent each individual must have those needs fulfilled to move up to the next level, so it is possible that just by recognizing and giving each person what each of us is capable of providing, in the way of fulfillment, we may be creating just the balance needed for another's upward move. This can sometimes be as simple as a welcome smile, a kind word, an understanding or listening ear, or spending time.

Let's see how it works for every human being, regardless of age, socio-economic level, etc. Our most basic needs are **physiological.** To insure our survival, we need food, shelter, sleep, liquid, and oxygen. Once our physical needs are satisfied, the need for **safety** emerges. Here we look to be safe from harm, injury or loss. The third level of need is for **love, affection, and belonging.** When these needs are satisfied, then the need for **esteem** arises. These needs include the desire for mastery, independence and respect for and from others.

MASLOW'S HIERARCHY OF NEEDS MODEL

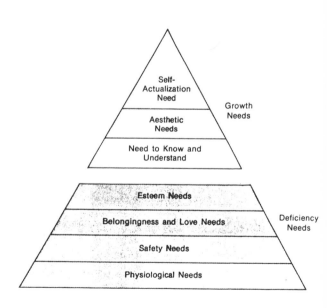

Maslow's Hierarchy of Needs

Maslow identifies two types of needs, deficiency needs and growth needs. People are motivated to satisfy needs at the bottom of the hierarchy before seeking those at the top.

Adapted from Maslow, 1954

Deficiency needs
Basic requirements for physical and psychological well-being, as identified by Maslow

Growth needs
Needs for knowing, appreciating, and understanding, which people try to satisfy after their basic needs are meet

Self-Actualization Need

Aesthetic Needs

Need to Know and Understand

Growth Needs

Esteem Needs

Belongingness and Love Needs

Safety Needs

Physiological Needs

Deficiency Needs

It is no accident that the schools in America are feeding the hungry, soothing the injured/abused, and purposely providing a safe environment for nurturing those who come under their charge. Education codes mandate that schools provide a "safe environment". If we expect that our students will learn, we <u>must</u> insure this **existence level** need. If we do not insure that this need is met, to some extent, the student will be hard pressed to concentrate upon the higher level needs, i.e. **achievement needs and self-actualization.** The same is true of the **relationship needs**. It is imperative that we include all students in the existing social environment developed in the classroom. To leave **anyone** out, regardless of any reasons we want to invent, is to insure a no-growth situation for that person in that setting, because one cannot concentrate on the higher levels, such as achievement, without a sense of belonging. It is only when all of the components are in place that human beings can move ahead, and grow and mature to be all that they can be. Without that insurance, we assist in developing anti-social behavior.It is clear that fulfillment of the need for esteem provides the transition from deficiency needs to growth needs. It is only then, with the fulfillment of esteem needs, that we develop the need to know and understand, aesthetic needs and upon occasion, the very top of the fulfillment pyramid, self-actualization.

In spite of the fact that educators and parents cannot be all things to all people, we can indeed provide the environment, the nurturing, and the ingredients it takes to create growth. Let's look at what it takes.

The Piggy Bank Theory of Self-Esteem
(adapted from Jack Canfield's Poker Chip Theory of Learning)

To illustrate how high and/or low self-esteem effects learning we will let a student's self-esteem be represented by pennies in a piggy bank. Some of our students today come into the world with very little in their piggy banks. We have crack babies, alcohol dependent babies, and babies of the poor and homeless. We have other babies who come into the world with many advantages. As youngsters are raised and grow they have different experiences based upon their socialization process. The fortunate students have lots of pennies in their banks due to academic success, social success, parental support, particular attractiveness, gifts and talents, high socio-economic levels, parents who have "made it" according to societal standards, and many more "fortunate" circumstances which may be apparent. As a result some students come to school with lots of pennies in their banks and some come with very few. Those with warm nurturing parents will undoubtedly have more pennies than students who were abused. Students who have had a chance to participate in educational experiences will have more in their bank than those who have never been exposed to story reading or the like. Those who have more are able and/or willing to risk more. Students are asked to risk every time the teacher gives an assignment. Each assignment has its own risk attached to it. To write a paper, recite poetry, create a work of art, answer a question in front of the class, or participate, cooperate, or share in any way. All have an inherent risk factor.

The student with high self-esteem will be more likely to participate than one with very low self-esteem. Those students who have fewer pennies in their banks will anxiously guard the few they have and simply not risk ridicule, censure, judgement, error, punishment, disapproval, rejection and at the deepest level, their self-esteem.

Those students with fewer pennies use "acting out" behavior and language that is considered inappropriate for the classroom. They says things like "This is stupid", "I won't do it", "This sucks". These things actually mean that the student is faced with a fear of being exposed. as "less" than someone else. Those things mean, "I am stupid", "I am afraid to try", "I have attempted this same lesson over and over and I have never gotten it right".. "Leave me alone."

We can all see why it is important to create activities and lessons in the classroom that allow all students to gain self-esteem so they will be willing to **participate and risk** in order to learn. We need to build in successes so that when students do make a mistake, they are more likely to learn from it and further enhance their self-esteem. If we want students to spend lots of pennies we need to help them build their bank accounts so they have lots of pennies to spend. The way to build a full piggy bank is to begin building daily successes.no matter how tiny. With each subsequent success comes the willingness to risk enough to build more.

WHY IS THIS SELF-ESTEEM THEORY IMPORTANT
IN THE CLASSROOM?

This model of learning theory is important in the classroom because it shows why some students refuse to participate in class discussions or activities. When students feel they have few pennies they know they are out of the "game", and no one wants to drop out or be kicked out of the "game". So rather than take the chance of losing all their pennies, they refuse to play. As teachers and parents we need to provide many ways for our students to add pennies to their banks so they will be more likely to participate in school and home/family activities. When the piggy bank account is full and someone ventures an attempt at something and they make an error, it will not bankrupt them. Students with high self-esteem not only take more risks academically and socially, they are also more likely to learn from their mistakes than those people with low self-esteem. The more pennies one has the easier it is to remain "in the game." So once again, the way to build a bank account, which leads to high self-esteem, is to build in deliberate and incremental successes on a day to day basis.

Because self-esteem is partially developed and nourished from a feeling you get from being connected to a deeper purpose, it is important to get beyond survival and at the least up to belonging, on Maslow's Hierarchy, and to develop enough reserves in the old piggy bank so that one can begin to think about "purpose" as a possibility for taking some risk.

A major problem that young people seem to have, which impacts strongly on their self-esteem, is in the area of communication. Many students tell me that often they just do not know how to "talk" to people. They are not understood and everything they say gets them in trouble. Is it any wonder that when parents come home and ask their children how things went at school the answer comes out a muffled "nothin'". Because we have all had this kind of experience to some degree or another, communication skills will be discussed in the next chapter.

CHAPTER 4

COMMUNICATION SKILLS:

USING ESTEEMING LANGUAGE TO ENHANCE OUR LIVES

CHAPTER 4

COMMUNICATION SKILLS: Using Esteeming Language To Enhance Our Lives

One of the best ways to build self-esteem is to teach and model **positive,** empowering **communication skills**. To have students participate in other types and areas of self-esteem building activities and then be "put down" verbally by parents, teachers and/or other students, effectively negates all the good developed by the activities practiced. There can be no doubt in anyone's mind that the style of communication skills someone uses in interacting with an individual helps to shape the view that others and the individual has of him/herself. If, for example, a person receives messages from a parent or teacher in a rough voice the majority of the time, the receiver/student thinks of him/herself as "deserving" rough treatment.   Therefore it gives "permission" for that person to conduct him/herself in a rough manner. It is a cycle of the "chicken and egg" story The same principle is in operation when we talk to ourselves.   So let's take a quick look at communication skills.

MESSAGES WE GIVE AND RECEIVE

Communication skills can be divided into two areas: There are messages we **give** to and **receive** from others and messages we **give** to ourselves.

43

The messages we give to ourselves are called **self-talk**. All people talk to themselves to some extent or another. There is that little voice that gives us messages about our looks, our behavior, our ability, our intelligence, our personality, etc.

COMMUNICATION USED WITH SELF: "SELF TALK"

The messages people give themselves have an enormous impact on their **self-esteem** and their **level of ability** to accomplish things. **As is our confidence, so is our capacity.** How many people have been told they could not do something and have told themselves that they **could** and simply moved ahead and done it? Reflect back to something you changed in your life by using self-talk. Maybe it was that you were no longer afraid of something or someone, or maybe it had to do with an accomplishment you achieved against some odds. Or maybe you told yourself that "living alone would be better than living in an abusive situation, and you could make it alone just fine". Whatever it was you achieved, you did so because you told yourself you could do it.

The same   result is true when we tell ourselves that we **cannot** do something. Our self-talk creates our reality. The old saying "whether you think you can or you think you can't, you are right" Many people, through using negative thoughts and language, have actually sabotaged and condemned themselves to a life of imprisonment without actually being behind bars. They walk around tired, hurt, angry, defensive, envious, holding a grudge, etc. All because they are allowing themselves negative thoughts and negative language.

It is important to understand the power of the human mind. When we teach students (and ourselves) to take charge of their own messages they begin to build a "winning" relationship with themselves. They begin to know that they are not "stuck" with the messages they have received thus far in their lives, because those old messages can be replaced with positive messages. With a belief in one's self, coupled with a few tangible life successes, one begins to really understand that anything is possible. It is a self-fulfilling prophecy. There are many examples we could use to illustrate this point.

Some of us were told we were sloppy as children and unless a life changing event occurred to us, such as leaving home, moving into your own apartment, dorm life at college, or getting married, we continue to be sloppy long into adulthood. We can also reflect on any number of things that work in the opposite way, things that affirm a gift or talent.

For example, my cousin John was always told he had tremendous musical talent. Through school he kept up the instrumental practice because he was sure that the messages he received had credence. Even though he thought he wanted to be an accountant and studied accounting in college guess what John missed studying in college? Although he did not get a degree in music, he now plays and writes music for motion pictures, and certainly chuckles when he takes his income tax to his accountant once a year, because John "knows" he is a good musician. Everyone told him that, and still does. I'll just bet John could have been a good accountant too.

THE SUBCONSCIOUS MIND

How does it all work? Let's discuss, for a brief moment, the subconscious mind. The subconscious mind is like a giant sponge that picks up and holds on to all the messages that it ever receives, from the time we are born, to the time we die. It's these messages which determine, to a great extent, how we act in life situations. If we perceive ourselves as shy, due to messages we have received or given ourselves to that effect, we are more likely to act shyly in a group than if our subconscious mind has received lots of messages affirming that we are outgoing. If we are given messages that we are fat or lazy and we tell ourselves those same things, we act in ways to make those messages true.

The subconscious mind cannot tell the difference between the truth (reality) and a lie (fantasy). For this reason, if we wish to change the image we have of our self, we can simply convince the subconscious mind, by our own self-talk, that we are outgoing. Therefore, we have a better chance of acting that way. Then once we have successfully acted outgoing, it becomes easier to act that way again until eventually, it (outgoingness) becomes our reality.

THE EFFECT OF NEGATIVE SELF-TALK
ON PHYSICAL STRENGTH:

Although most everyone talks to themselves, there is a qualitative difference in the way people do that. Just as some people are very gentle, and some people are very rough when they speak to others, the same is true when people talk to themselves. The problem is, however, that even those people who are

46

gentle with others are sometimes very punishing with themselves. For example, let's take that little voice that points out, harshly, when we forget our dentist appointment, or to pick up something at the store, or to call and cancel an appointment we are unable to keep. Does your voice bombard you with statements like, " Oh, I just can't remember anything these days", Or "I must be getting old, I forget twice as much as I used to", Or "Boy am I a screw-up again. Now I have to pay for an appointment for nothing", Or "Boy, This time I really blew it. Nobody will trust me again.". Whatever the negative messages are that we communicate to ourselves without thinking much about them, are often draining our strength and energy.

There is a demonstration that shows clearly how negative self-talk drains physical energy. Literally our physical strength is sapped from our bodies when we engage in negative thoughts and communication. To summarize this sample activity or demonstration: A volunteer holds an arm out to their side and someone stands behind them and tries to push the arm down while the volunteer resists. After it has been established that the arm cannot be pushed down without considerable effort, the volunteer is instructed to repeat four or five times aloud, "My right arm is very weak". The volunteer can then hold her/his arm out and resist.. Without fail, it will be easier to push the arm down, sometimes so much easier that the volunteer will be shocked. The volunteer then says aloud four or five times, "I have a very strong and powerful right arm", and holds out the "strong and powerful right arm". He/she resists once again and their arm appears stronger once more when pushed down. This clearly demonstrates how powerful positive self-talk can be in terms of creating physical strength. So, negative self-talk not only sabotages one's emotional and mental well being, it can also drain one's physical strength.

This same "arm test" can be done a second time and the person holding out the arm can discover how **negative internal thoughts** do the same thing. The first time will show how **negative** language used **aloud**, drains physical energy. For the second go around, have the volunteer lower his chin to his chest and **think** of an event that was sad, embarrassing, or shameful. The arm will be in a weakened state. The arm will be very much strengthened if the person gets a reward or acknowledgment of some sort, such as a standing ovation, and then attempts to hold his arm out straight while it is being pushed. Once the standing ovation is accomplished, the arm regains its strength.

The impact of this demonstration must not be underestimated. Most people have never given consideration to the way they have control over their own strength. Do not be surprised if people are disbelieving. Let them be skeptical and invite them to try the same exercise with friends, students and family members. The same type of results will occur in the arm test when a happy or sad face, is projected with an overhead projector. Think of the impact a facial expression makes on children when we approach them.

The same principle is true when we repeatedly say we feel sick. That type of message increases our feelings of weakness and illness. How is it that some people take so little sick leave and others are often out sick, even though they have experienced the same weather conditions or the same exposure to viruses. Some people, at the earliest sign of a sniffle, begin to tell themselves how sick they feel. Our subconscious gets the signal and says "Oh! Oh, time to start making me sick." If the voice-mind can get negative control, it will. We have a tendency to sabotage our own lives by our own negative talk. One of the major effects of self-talk is that it gives us control over the choices we make. If we continually tell ourselves we are not deserving, we will undoubtedly make choices that fulfill this prophecy. The same is true about positive self-fulfilling prophecy. **Talk to yourself, by all means, and let the messages be positive, nurturing, and empowering.**

COMMUNICATION USED WITH OTHERS

In order to build self-esteem in yourself and others you need to have communication patterns which are **positive, nurturing, and empowering.** It is especially important for teachers and parents to model the kind of language patterns we want our students and children to use in order to learn how to take responsibility for themselves. In order to produce the results we want them to achieve, it is our job to first show them, through our own usage, that there is language which empowers.

One of the most powerful tools that a person has at his or her fingertips is the ability to **ward off negative comments** made by others. Although this is not an easy thing to learn to do, with ample practice one **can** learn not to internalize a put down, insult or negative comment. How? Simply say to the person who is doing the put down, "Thank you for sharing your opinion". This has the power to neutralize the effect of the negative comment's intent and allows the receiver to ward it off. The reason that the negative comment is rendered harmless is because your mind is clear that it is only an opinion and not in any way a fact. Everybody is entitled to their opinions. It will amaze you how effective this technique really is. Now all we need is to practice using this technique.

Sometimes the language we use to express ourselves is just as damaging as the negative language used toward us. The way we speak can turn us into victims.

VICTIM VS. POWERFUL (OR EMPOWERING) LANGUAGE (LEMERES)

Several examples of victim vs. powerful (or empowering) language as conceived by Clare Lemeres are as follows:

VICTIM: I **have** to go to school...
POWERFUL: I **choose** to go to school.

VICTIM: I **can't** get to school on time...
POWERFUL: I **don't** get to school on time.

VICTIM: I am **trying** to get things done...
POWERFUL: I am **getting** things done.

VICTIM: It's **not my fault**...
POWERFUL: I am totally **responsible.**

VICTIM: **If only**...
POWERFUL: **Next time ---**

VICTIM: I **should**...
POWERFUL: I **could ---**

VICTIM: It's a **problem...**
POWERFUL: It's an **opportunity** and a **challenge!**

Using this "victim" language may seem to be harmless or merely a matter of semantics. Don't be fooled by how it looks to you. It is very demoralizing to allow your subconscious mind the opportunity to dwell in negative territory. How many other examples of this type of "victim" language do you have running through your own vocabulary and communication patterns? What can you do to get rid of them?

I. Take note of how often you use negative/victim language.
2. Acknowledge yourself for catching it.
3. Simply rephrase it
4. Celebrate your ability to break an old habit. That is not easy to do.
5. Remember to allow yourself to "blow it" as often as you do. That keeps the challange ever present.

FROM VICTIM TO VICTOR:

In order for students, and adults to grow and change from **victim to victor** it is necessary for teachers and parents to acknowledge:
1. Faith in a student's **ability** to learn, grow, and change behavior.
2. That it is certain and **possible** for a student to improve in any area of life.
3. That the **locus of control** in students is **internal**.
4. That they can take **responsibility** for their own learning and life circumstances.

Ask your students, your children, and yourselves the following questions:
Who is in charge of you?
Who is in charge of your perceptions?
Who is in charge of your thoughts?
Who determines what you **choose** to think?

For many people, (parents, students, and teachers), a huge amount of time is spent thinking they have no power or control over their own lives and destiny. The above communication piece is designed to get people to think about giving away their power. They can think about to whom they give their power, and why. Asking these questions will also keep them in touch with the reality and importance of internal locus of control.

AFFIRMATIONS and VISUALIZATIONS

Another way to gain empowerment is through **affirmations and visualizations.** An **affirmation** is a specific statement made to describe a behavior or condition which one would like to acquire. A **visualization** is simply a mind picture of a behavior or condition one wishes to acquire. As I said earlier, doing daily affirmations is a great way to change many of the negative internal tapes that we have going. There are many affirmations teachers can design to illustrate the above points. Better yet, let the students design affirmations for their personal ownership and longer lasting effect.

Creating affirmations is also a way to get students to analyze and evaluate areas of their lives which they personally deem needs improving. This self study helps to keep them in touch with their real selves in a non-defensive way.

Here is a quick overview of how affirmations are done and several examples of affirmations.

STEP 1   Affirmations are done to **change** or modify a condition already present or to achieve a desired condition.

STEP 2   Affirmations are done in the **present tense**, as though the desired condition has already been achieved.

STEP 3   Affirmations are done on a **daily basis,** once or more preferably the first thing in the morning or the last thing at night. This is a more relaxing time.

STEP 4   Affirmations are preferably to be done **out loud**. If that makes you uncomfortable, do them in your head

STEP 5   Affirmations are to be done in front of a **mirror**.

STEP 6   Affirmations are done until the desired **condition** is **achieved.**

EXAMPLES: Let's suppose someone has difficulty doing multiplication problems or a variety of other things. That person would use the above formula, and say:

"Every time I work on multiplication, I understand it clearly and can figure out the correct answer."

"I am doing homework every day, and having a great time learning, and taking responsibility for my own learning success."

"Each time I have a negative thought, I notice it, and quickly turn it into a positive one, creating my own happiness."

"Every day I am getting thinner and thinner."

"I am punctual, enthusiastic, and prepared for each meeting I attend."

"I am in a wonderful relationship with a warm, sensitive, caring man who loves me just the way I am."

People can design affirmations for any and every condition we wish to address and change. Some of my favorites are as follows: **"As I go through today and every day I ....**
...am so strong that nothing can disturb my peace of mind.
...talk health, happiness and prosperity to every person I meet.
...make all my friends feel that they are worthwhile and appreciated.
...look at the positive side of things and make my optimism reality.
...am committed to excellence in my teaching, and for my students.
...am as enthusiastic about the success of others as I am about my own
...forget the mistakes of the past and create greater achievements for the future.
...dedicate so much time to the improvement of all of my projects.

Affirmations do not work overnight as some people would like them to, but, given enough time and attention, they really do work. I know that from personal experience. It is through affirmations that I met my wonderful husband. That is a story for another time.

Once we can show students how empowering it is to take responsibility for their own decisions, about what they affirm for themselves, they will begin to "claim" their lives in a variety of ways, especially in the learning process. **Taking personal responsibility is one of the primary ingredients for gaining high self-esteem.** The more practice a person has in this area the more natural a part of daily life it becomes. **It is a winner-builder.**

ASSERTIVE COMMUNICATION SKILLS

The author of <u>Teacher Effectiveness Training</u> (TET) and <u>Parent Effectiveness Training</u> (PET) is Dr. Thomas Gordon. He has a wonderful communication model for giving clear messages and making your feelings and needs known so that the person to whom you are speaking can really **hear** your message. The two major techniques that Gordon feels make an effective teacher or parent are **I-messages and Active listening.**

I-messages and Active Listening are methods of **clarifying communication** because they allow one to tell others how one feels and what one needs or wants. These techniques allow one to determine how others feel and what they want as well. That way one has the opportunity to **control** those things for which he/she is **responsible**, and to **relinquish the control** to the appropriate party for those things for which he/she is not responsible. Through this method of communication people become able to tell the difference about the whole issue of responsibility.

A person can make choices about how he/she chooses to behave based on the needs and wants of others and him/herself. This responsibility directed behavior enhances the self-esteem of both parties. People begin to feel **listened to** and **heard**.

I-messages are the principle way that we can have our needs met through the communication process. They are the **assertive** way we tell other people that their behavior is disturbing us in some way without being aggressive, angry, or intimidating.

I-messages consist of three parts:
1. One's **feelings** about a particular behavior.
2. A **description** of the **behavior** causing the difficulty. (Be sure that you emphasize the behavior not the person).
3. The **change** in the behavior you would like to see take place.

For example a teacher might say,

"I feel irritated when I have to shout to be heard when I am giving directions. I need to have it quiet at those times."

Once you have given an **I-message**, you have to be ready to listen to the person or persons receiving the message because they may have some feelings to discuss when they find out their behavior is causing you some difficulty. The best way to do this is with a technique called **Active Listening**. The main idea behind **Active Listening** is that the listener will encourage the speaker to express his/her feelings and possible courses of action. The speaker, who gave the original I-message, has now become the active listener who will actively encourage the receiver to explore courses of action, and come to a decision about how to handle the request. It is not possible to gain satisfaction instantly with this method of communication. It takes a great deal of practice to become proficient at it. In the meantime you will begin to reap rewards for your efforts because your interpersonal relationships will begin to improve along with your technique.

There are a number of books available on these two communication techniques, the best of which are I-messages and active listening. It is necessary, as with any new technique to practice, practice, practice, until you can really give clear I-messages and engage in the kind of active listening which promotes others to open up to you in a non-defensive manner. The rewards far outweigh the time it takes to use this method of communication.

PRAISING AND ENCOURAGEMENT

Another way to build self-esteem in students is by **praising.** Both in the classroom and at home we often use praise to acknowledge students for the good things they do. In order for praise to be **effective** and build and enhance self-esteem it must have certain qualities to it. It goes far beyond the idea that you say, "Good job", no matter what the attempt looks like.

Rudolph Dreikers says, "Children need encouragement, just as plants need water. They can not survive without it." Teachers and parents can make a world of difference when they focus on the positives in areas of encouragement. The wrong kind of praise can produce anxiety, insecurity, and misbehavior, while the proper type of praise can be a magic wand. Correctly practiced, praise **supports** children and **encourages confidence, capabilities, security, and persistence.**

Let's look at some of the ways that praise can best be handled to maximize its effect in a positive and esteeming fashion. These guidelines from Stephanie Marston will help in the use of praise both at home and at school.

1. Focus on the actual efforts and achievements the student makes rather than on character traits.

School   "You have certainly put lots of effort into learning the skills (be specific) you have acquired in math."

Home   "You really put lots of effort into cleaning and organizing you room."

2. Be Specific

School   "I like the way you stayed on task all period today."

Home   "I like the way you put all of your toys in your toy box."

3. Express how you feel about what a student has done.

School   "I feel excited when you demonstrate how much you have learned about writing good paragraphs."

Home   "I feel encouraged when you demonstrate such responsible behavior."

4. Let the person you are praising draw positive conclusions about him/herself.

School   "How do you feel about your successful efforts?"

Home   "How do you feel about your successful efforts?"

5.   Focus on progress and effort in your encouragement.

School   "You have really taken responsibility for studying and learning the components and organization of the short story."

Home   "You have certainly taken responsibility for pitching in and doing your share of the family chores."

6.   After the praise, stop talking and let the person being praised take it in and internalize it.

It is a great idea to solicit from students, as much as possible, ways of self-acknowledgement. This allows them to be their own evaluator and they are more liable to set their own high standards, while noticing that they are responsible for their own success.   This is a way to encourage them in esteeming themselves.   It is most important that students get to the place where they are able to evaluate the positive outcomes for themselves whenever they have them.   That allows them to weigh both successful attempts and to look forward to doing things again if the end result is not the desired result.

CELEBRATING MISTAKES

The majority of people in this world are socialized to believe that **mistakes** are "bad" or "wrong". Some people feel defensive and rationalize their mistakes. Some people are so afraid they will be judged poorly that they can never admit having made an error. Other people become depressed and incapacitated over errors because they strive to appear to be the picture of perfection. In fact, many people would rather sacrifice almost anything, including their health and well-being, rather than admit they are "wrong" about something.

Allowing for mistakes as **catalysts to learning** is a very important concept to infuse in children and in ourselves as well. Nobody is perfect, which in itself is perfect, because it is the leveler that allows us to have a sense of belonging. It is only when people cover up their mistakes in order to appear to be more perfect than others, that guilt and a lack of self-esteem gain a foothold. Teaching youngsters and adults to use their errors as a **growth** and **improvement** tool by first **admitting** the error, then **evaluating** how and why it happened, and **determining** how to "revisit" or "redo" the mistake, does several things to improve the initial outcome. **An opportunity** is gained to look for a different and creative way to an expected outcome. Also, any critic who may be ready to pounce on them for the mistake is disarmed. It is also a catalyst to gaining inner personal strength, and allowing more healthy risk taking, while knowing that one's life and reputation does not hang in the balance of having to be "perfect". Human beings have the opportunity to relax a bit, strive to be their personal best, and equip themselves to "regroup" if things do not go as planned or intended. Many educators find this idea difficult because they have a vested interest in being "right" almost always, therefore it is difficult for students to find role models to demonstrate that mistakes can be seen in a positive light.

Teaching students to **reframe** mistakes is an important part of the growth process. How much more constructive it is to accept ourselves unconditionally as inherently worthy beings, acknowledge our errors, learn from them and move on, using the newly found knowledge to do a better job the next time, knowing that every error brings us closer to the desired outcome. If we could teach youngsters to look at mistakes **as a necessary part of the learning process**, as merely **information about what does work and what doesn't**, as simply **necessary steps to reaching a goal**, we would have less fearful human beings. We could simply notice that given a second crack at it, they might choose to do it differently. We could even learn to celebrate our mistakes because without them we would not be as far along the path to the next success. Thomas Edison made hundreds of "mistakes" before he invented the light bulb. If he had been upset with his "mistakes" at any time along his path to success, if he had simply quit because he couldn't do it "right" the first time, if people thought of his mistakes as a sign that he couldn't do it right over and over and over, we would all be sitting in darkness.

Changing Communication Patterns: Difficult, Possible, Necessary, and Very Worthwhile.

Because language is a learned behavior, it is very difficult to modify and change the language patterns we have established over the years. Most of us do not ever begin to realize what effect language has on our self-image and on the image others have of us. In order to effect a change, a person must be aware of his/her own communication patterns. One must also be committed to the effort and hard work it takes to make the changes.

To encourage students to change the language patterns they use teachers must first demonstrate empowering changes. It may mean backing up and re-doing some of the messages that are sent. That requires taking a risk. You may find yourself saying, "That was a negative statement. Let me say that again differently." The results will be well worth it. You will re-learn more positive language and re-create your own image, and best of all you will model for your students, your children, and others that it is okay to make errors and admit them, and that it is hard work and valuable work to keep positive messages going out to others. Because students learn best by our modeling, once students hear our language modeling, they will begin to adjust and modify their own language. It is important to point out the changes to students so that they can have an opportunity to practice making their own changes. The **change** process is predicated on three factors: **Awareness, Commitment, and Action.**

Detours To Roadblocks To Communication

There are many ways that people set up roadblocks to the communication process. There is a list of roadblocks that Dr. Thomas Gordon suggests in Parent Effectiveness Training, an excellent book for every parent to have around as a reference source. Dr. Gordon says:

    ordering, directing, commanding
    warning, admonishing, threatening
    moralizing, preaching, obliging
    advising, giving suggestions or solutions
    judging, criticizing, disagreeing, blaming
    name calling, ridiculing, shaming

are the things that get in the way of true communication.

As an example many teachers and parents set up roadblocks to communication by **telling** students **how** to solve their problems instead of allowing them to find ways to solve the problems themselves. By **noticing** each time you start to tell a student how to solve his/her problem you have taken the first step toward changing that communication pattern. Sometimes it is helpful to tell the students what changes you are trying to make in your own behavior and why, and ask them if they would be willing to help you make the changes by noticing, along with you, when you start to **tell** them how to solve their problem. If you are committed to making a change, then you will use every opportunity to **rephrase** your communications so that they will accomplish what you want. The act of rephrasing is one action you can take to help create a change. Another action you can take is **guided practice** in a role-playing situation with someone willing to help. You can also use your subconscious mind to help you change. By using affirmations and/or visualizations you can increase your ability to affect changes in your communication patterns. It takes time and commitment to make changes.

Awareness, affirmations, visualizations, and practice will insure your goal for change.

We could learn the power of the words we think and say to our selves.
We could learn how to create positive self-talk.
We could model the use of positive self-talk
We could use self-responsible language patterns and empowering language for ourselves and others.
Replace "I can't" with "I can", or "I won"t".
Replace "I'll try" with "I will".

Replace "should" with "want to" or "don"t want to".

We could make affirmations to change conditions we wish to change.

We could use assertive communication skills to express our feelings.

We could actively listen so others will know we really hear them.

We could keep a positive, success-oriented focus.

We could use encouragement when responding to "wrong"answers.

We could practice visualizing the successes we want to achieve.

We could set goals and celebrate the steps we take that lead to success.

We could allow ourselves to empower others by using language patterns that enhance and esteem

We could remember that every human being is lovable, capable and worthwhile.

CHAPTER 5

DECISION-MAKING AND CONFLICT RESOLUTION:

AN OPPORTUNITY FOR EMPOWERMENT

CHAPTER 5

<u>**DECISION-MAKING/CONFLICT RESOLUTION:**</u>
<u>**An Opportunity For Empowerment**</u>

People have the opportunity to make many decisions and solve many problems. Most of us make these choices from an **emotional base** rather than from a well thought out **organized plan** which promotes **positive choices.** Often people base their choices on how they feel about themselves and their needs. If they have high self-esteem they are more likely to make positive choices because they trust their own innate feelings and inner sense of self and have a built-in system for making organized choices. If their self-esteem is low, it is likely that choices are not based on what is "good" for the individual, partially because that low esteemed individual does not feel deserving of what is "good".

Choices for this group of individuals is based upon things outside of the self need, things like - "What would my buddies want me to do", "what can I get back if I do this", "Will people like me better (or less) if I do this", "I could really show so and so, if I did that", and other such **externally** motivated decisions. These types of decision making techniques leave the person **"at effect"** in his/her environment. The following information illustrates ways to provide individuals the opportunity to be **"at cause"** rather than at effect.

One of the ways to build self-esteem in students is to give them a sense of **empowerment**. The key to acquiring this power is for them to be aware that they have the ability to choose, perhaps not always **what** happens to them, but at least **how they react** to what happens to them. There are several ways to react to life situations. Students can react **aggressively, either verbally or physically.** This is not very esteeming because it usually hurts someone else. Students can react **passively**, essentially accepting a situation they do not like or ignoring that it exists. This is not esteeming because the students are hurting themselves. Students can react **passively on the outside and aggressively on the inside** so that they wait for a chance to gain revenge. This is not esteeming because the negative energy involved hurts everyone. **None of these reactions are good for a student's self-esteem.**

In order for students to develop a sense of **empowerment and responsibility** they need to understand that **they are responsible for their behavior and their feelings.** They need to know that because they are responsible for their behavior and their feelings they can make choices about them. If someone says, "You are a cheater," we can choose how we feel about that and we can choose how we will react to that statement. We could choose to feel hurt and angry and retaliate by calling them a liar, or we could choose to wonder why they are calling us a cheater and ask them why they think this is so. As teachers and parents we can point out these choices to our students whenever we get a chance and ask them to evaluate which choices would be the most positive for them.

Students need to learn to be **proactive** and prepared to handle any situation that comes along, both in school and in life. Teaching students a **process** through which they can make positive choices will encourage even students with low self-esteem to recognize **how to make positive choices, how to evaluate consequences, and** if the choices are not satisfactory, **how to choose again.**

Positive Choices

When we consider the value of **positive choices** we see that they help people get what they really want, they do not create consequences which hurt others or themselves, and they match people's beliefs and values. As students become aware that they do have choices and are allowed to evaluate the ones they make, they begin to acquire power over situations in their lives. Acquisition of this kind of power builds their self-esteem. Any writing activity or life activity in which the students are given a situation in which they respond with a choice can be used as an opportunity for evaluating their responses or choices according to the guidelines. There are proactive activities in a curriculum designed by the Community Board Program, Inc. They provide not only food for thought but an opportunity to do some problem solving with no one correct answer.

Students need to be aware that **being responsible for their behavior and their feelings** does not mean that they will always do the right thing, behave the right way, or feel good all the time. It does mean that they will have a way of **evaluating their actions and their feelings themselves so they can make a choice to act differently if the situation arises again and/or to act responsibly if their actions cause a problem for someone else.**

Developing a sense of empowerment in the area of **building relationships** is a very important part of our students' lives. While there are many aspects of building relationships, the area where most of us have difficulty is when there is confrontation or conflict. When we can keep the process of solving problems non-personal, and treat it like a challenge akin to solving a mystery, we begin to develop the distance and perspective needed to make a difference in the outcomes.

We talked earlier about how I-Messages and Active Listening can help students indicate that they are having a problem with someone else's behavior and how they can discover exactly what the problem is.

Now let's discuss how our students can solve the problems which arise, in a way that builds the self-esteem of both parties. The process contains eight steps and may seem rather difficult to use, but it is actually quite easy to use. In many cases not all the steps are needed.

This **model can be used to make decisions** for an individual or a group. It can also be **used to resolve conflicts** in the classroom and in the home as well. This model is **based on the esteem building assumption that students are responsible people,** like teachers, and parents, who want to and can solve any problem they encounter. There are as many or more good and equitable decisions and discipline solutions coming from students learning how to "solve their own problems" than there are from adults. First of all, the student "owns" the problem more when he/she is expected to come up with a solution to fit time, place, needs, equity, fairness, and agreement. Secondly, they begin to see how difficult it is to actually deal with problems themselves. This gives them an opportunity to build responsibility.

In order to have students succeed in this, teachers and parents need to come from the position or mind-set that students are **responsible and capable** of solving their own problems.

The following steps are important to follow in a decision making or problem solving model:

1. **Define** the problem
2. **Brainstorm** possible solutions or decisions
3. **Develop** consequences of each solution or decision
4. **Rate** the possibilities
5. **Pick** a solution to use, and use it
6. **Determine** how to evaluate and modify solutions
7. **Celebrate** positive results
8. **Evaluate** improvement possibilities

It is important to **spend time and energy thoroughly investigating the alternatives.** The more you learn about the options beforehand, the less uncertain you will be. Of course, you can't learn everything you need to know before deciding, so you also rely on the second way to reduce risk.

Evaluate the results of decisions. Were the goals met? Were the costs and benefits what you had anticipated? If the benefits were greater or the costs lower, there's no problem. But if the costs were more or the benefits less, you may want to change the decision, perhaps trying another alternative.

Evaluate how the decision was made. Was the problem, defined too narrowly? Did you overlook any options? Did you fail to see all the costs and benefits of each alternative? Did you take too much time to decide? By evaluating how well you decided, you can help yourself make better decisions in the future.

Decision making, problem solving, conflict resolution

The same model used for making decisions and solving problems can also be used to resolve conflicts with only slight modifications. There are many models for this process, however they all have a common thread. There is an element of **responsibility** on the part of all parties to work toward a **consensus solution,** or at least one which all parties are willing to accept. This builds the self-esteem of everyone involved, as well as provides a reason for everyone to help make the solution work. It is vital that students be given models to make decisions because they will have only themselves to depend upon at times. They need to feel empowered, in control, and proud to be able to work out their own problems. Students need to experience a willingness to accept the consequences of their personal decisions. This will assist them in "owning" the problem from the start.

Making the party or parties with whom the problem is occurring an integral part of the solution, so both can "get to yes", is a conflict resolution tool that really works a majority of the time. Reaching some acceptable compromise is esteeming to both parties. It can serve to bring people closer and it can help them better understand each other's needs. There are hundreds of examples any teacher or parent can use in the classroom or home for practicing problem-solving. The important thing is to invite the students to assist in solving problems together with the teacher or parent. Numbers of discipline problems will disappear, and the students will feel like it is truly their own learning environment.

With the emphasis on cooperative learning in schools today and on cooperative management structures in the business world and in the family, it is important for our students to see and learn the steps used to solve group problems and individual conflicts as well. Reaching solutions by consensus rather than by authority or manipulation is much more esteem building and is conducive with expectations in the world outside the school and family. Teachers and parents will be encouraged by the results and be more willing to continue to give all of the expertise, caring, and love that they give on a day-to-day basis.

It is very important to allow students to participate in the problem solving that goes on in a classroom and in a family. They will feel like they count, like they are intelligent when a solution is found, and they will be involved in the ownership of their classroom and home experience. Once again, this promotes active, not passive students; students who will be armed with the techniques you have modeled when they go on to other classes, become involved in community action, and begin to raise their own children. Each of these types of activities takes time, but the end product is an increased number of young people who feel great about their ability to make decisions in collaboration with others and on their own. This is one perfect way to begin to raise self-esteem--both your own and that of your students'. One of the many bonuses is that there will be far fewer discipline problems in your classrooms and in your homes.

This also gives students a reason and an opportunity to learn what it means to assume responsibility. As we move into this area of responsibility we have moved closer to completing the cycle of how teachers and parents can assist students in becoming esteemed individuals who, in turn, can make their own contributions to the world at large.

I am including one example of what we have been discussing so that it can be followed step by step using any problem. The one being used here is merely an example of how the model can work in school.

Let's take a look at a real life classroom problem as an example to help understand the different parts of the problem solving (or decision making or conflict resolution) process.

Problem Solving Model: From the Classroom of Ken Gelatt, Davis High School

"I was having trouble with my sixth period Algebra I class. They were very noisy and inattentive when I gave instructions, directions, and explanations. This was annoying me and a lot of the students were asking me the same questions again and again about the directions, or they were doing the activity or assignment incorrectly. Both the students and I were getting frustrated and learning had almost ceased. I wondered how to approach the class without being angry.

I decided to try giving them an "I-message," indicating that I had a problem. I said, 'I feel very frustrated when I give directions and it is noisy in the room because I have to give the directions over and over and there are still people who don't understand what to do' (I feel ... when... because...)

Then I waited for several of the students to respond to this message and I listened and accepted all of their responses. I received statements like:

"So what!"

"Yeah, I can't hear you. Why don't you make the class be quiet."

"I'm frustrated too because I don't know what you want us to do."

I then said, "Do you agree that we have a problem that we need to solve?" The majority of the class agreed. Then I asked them if they would be willing to try a problem-solving process that might help us solve our problem. They agreed so we began the process.

Define the problem or decision or conflict

The first step was fairly easy in this case. We agreed on the problem. There was too much noise and too little attention when I was giving directions.

Brainstorm possible solutions or decisions together

I opened the discussion by explaining that in brainstorming any idea was allowed, and that no judgements or put downs were to be made about any solution no matter what. The following is a sampling of the solutions we generated:

> *Institute point penalties for students who are talking*
> *Don't give directions aloud. Write them on the board.*
> *Give them anyway and don't answer any questions afterward.*
> *Don't give any directions until the whole class is quiet.*

I wrote these on the board and asked a student to copy them for us because the period was about to end. I gave them a review assignment for that night and they all listened to the directions. The next day I quickly reviewed what we had accomplished and what parts of the problem-solving process we had used. Then we proceeded to the next step.

Develop the consequences of each solution or decision.

We decided on the consequences for each of the following solutions:

Point penalties were very negative and they made the teacher into a policeman who spent a lot of time keeping track of who lost points. There would also be a lot of arguing by students who felt they were not talking or that they were being singled out unfairly.

Not giving the directions out loud but writing them on the board created a lot of work for the teacher and in some cases the directions were too complicated to write.

Giving the directions anyway and not answering any questions did not ease my frustration of having to talk over a noisy classroom nor did it ease the students' frustration of not knowing what to do. The consequence of this possibility was that the problem would not be solved.

Not giving directions until the whole class was quiet would possibly solve the problem of the noisy classroom but it would take a lot of time to wait for the class to be quiet and it would not solve the difficulty of those students who did not understand the directions.

After listing these consequences we proceeded to the next step.

Rate the possibilities together

After very little discussion we rated the solutions as follows:
1. Wait until the whole class was quiet.
2. Point penalties.
3. Write the directions on the board.
4. Give them anyway and answer no questions.

The next step was to pick a solution that everyone could accept. If one person was not happy with the solution it could not be used. This included the teacher. This is decision by consensus. (It is important to realize that the solution you pick is not permanent and that you don't have to get the best or the "right" solution the first time.)

Pick a solution

We all vetoed number 4 and I vetoed number 2 because I did not want to be so negative or do so much work. I also was not willing to write all my directions on the board or an overhead projector, as someone added while we were discussing this solution. That left number 1 and I asked if there was anyone who objected to that solution. Since no one objected I also agreed to accept it although I really didn't want to waste so much time because I felt some people would not get quiet quickly enough. Now we were ready for the last step.

Determine how to evaluate the solution or decision and how to modify it later if necessary

We decided that anyone who felt that the solution wasn't working should indicate that to the teacher and we would hold another class discussion on how to modify the solution.

As you might have guessed it didn't take long for us to realize that it was not working. The first couple of times I tried to give directions I waited about 30 seconds but when I began to talk many students started to talk also. After two days I said that I felt the solution wasn't working. Many of the class members agreed.

At this point we could have repeated the process to see if we could generate different solutions but that didn't seem to me to be too profitable. Then I used an idea that provided some extra information that allowed us to generate a solution that worked reasonably well for the rest of the year. _The idea was to ask the students if they could help by deciding how they would like directions or explanations given._

I asked each student to take out a sheet of paper and write how they preferred directions or explanations to be given and what types of things made this difficult. I collected the papers and read them between classes. It seemed that about 75% of the class felt that I took too long to give my directions or that I explained the same thing over and over. Most of them got it the first time through and yet I kept repeating the instructions, as some teachers are prone to do. (Very bright students suffer through this on a daily basis. It is, in fact, the reason so many very bright students opt to drop out of school. They feel that their time is being wasted by too much talk and too little action.)

I was excited to have found the key to solving the problem. Armed with this new information, I suggested the following solution. If they would be quiet, then I would take only two minutes or less to give my directions and 10 minutes or less to give my explanations. They all agreed to this and even though we both did not always follow through, we were able to solve the problem together. An added bonus was that we all felt closer and worked better after this process."

This successful model can be used in the home and in the work place as well. Other teachers have reported remarkable results in many areas of their teaching responsibilities. Several parents with whom I have worked have told me that it changed the relationship they had with their children for the better when they used this model. Making the party or parties with whom the problem is occurring an integral part of the solution, so both can "get to yes", is a conflict resolutions tool that really works a majority of the time. Reaching compromise is esteeming to both parties. It can serve to bring people closer and it can help them better understand each other's needs.

This example is only one of hundreds any teacher or parent can use in the classroom. The important thing is to **invite the students to assist in solving the problems together with the teacher or the parent.** The number of discipline problems will almost disappear, the students will feel like it is truly **their own learning and/or home environment,** and the teacher and/or parent will be encouraged to continue to give all of the expertise, caring, and love he/she has to give on a day to day basis.

CHAPTER 6

ASSUMING RESPONSIBILITY:

TAKING CHARGE — AN ESTEEMING PROCESS

CHAPTER 6

ASSUMING RESPONSIBILITY:
Taking Charge - An Esteeming Process

Being Responsible

Being responsible means **accepting** the fact that you have **control** over your actions, feelings, and perceptions. Every person has control over their behavior, choices, time priorities, care of their body, the relationships they choose to develop, continue, or terminate, the way they react to or are pro-active about life situations, the way they feel about and respond to themselves and others.

Being responsible does not mean taking the "blame" or feeling guilty for actions or feelings of others.

Being responsible means that:

1. You recognize those aspects of your life over which you have control.
2. You have the ability to recognize how you interrelate to everything in your environment.
3. You make choices about how to use your control
4. You are willing to accept consequences or the outcome for both positive and negative choices you make.

Consequences fall in to two types, natural and logical. **Natural consequences** happen as a result of choices we make or behaviors that we exhibit. For example, if we fall into a swimming pool, we get wet. If we fall down a flight of stairs, we get bruised, etc. **Logical consequences** are set up by someone else, of any age or position of authority. Logical consequences are"logical" only if they are reasonable and respectful to both parties and are related to the behavior.

The fact that Tommy does not have his homework done is not a matter of irresponsibility in itself. If Tommy accepts the fact that he chose to do something other than finish the homework and is willing to **accept the consequences**, then he is acting responsibly according to his needs and should be acknowledged for it. Maybe Tommy's older brother was home from college and since Tommy knew the material he decided that he could afford to miss this assignment in order to spend time with his brother.

Sam feels sad because Maria would rather stay home Friday night than go to the game with him. Sam goes to the game alone and does not have a good time. The next day he does not speak to Maria because he is mad at her for ruining his evening. Maria is not responsible for the way Sam feels. Sam needs to take responsibility for his feelings. Only he can control how he feels at the game. Sam needed to **choose to feel differently** if he wanted to have a good time at the game.

Bill scored very poorly on his math test. He did not finish all the problems. While he was studying for the test he realized that he did not understand the material, but he did not look for extra help from the teacher prior to the test. After the test he complains loudly that the teacher was unfair and the test was no good. He thinks he should be allowed to make up the test.

Showing Bill where his responsibility begins and where the teacher's responsibility begins and ends will help Bill learn to take responsibility in the future when this type of opportunity occurs. The types of questions a teacher or parent would direct to Bill are important for the learning process. There must be no blame. Bill needs to process the problem with a greater sense of awareness about the issue of where his responsibility begins and ends.

Empowerment comes through being responsible.

It is important to teach students the relationship between cause and effect. With reponsibility comes privilege. When we do not exhibit responsible behavior, the effect may not be what we want it to be.

Give students opportunities to be responsible.

Any time a teacher or parent can help students solve their own problems they are developing responsibility in the youngster. Use of active listening and I-messages will help them discover responsible behavior. Parents and teachers (and many others in positions of power) often have difficulty empowering others due to their fear of lack of control. When someone has confidence in another's ability to be responsible, they usually discover that they have placed their confidence wisely.

Let students help set the guidelines or operating procedures for the class or home. Also have them create the consequences for exhibiting irresponsibility. Allow students to have a say in what the outcome will be if they choose not to be responsible. Help young people deal with the consequences when they don't behave in a responsible fashion. The **behavior, not the person,** must be the focus of concern.

Do not give students lots of responsibility all at once. Let them **practice** in small increments so that when they are successful with a small task they can be allowed and **encouraged** to take and **assume** more responsibility.

Help students deal with the consequences when they don't behave responsibly

1. **Do not judge their behavior.** Simply assist them in getting back on track toward being responsible once again.
2. We all fail to accomplish something at one time or another. A student frequently becomes very upset when he/she acts irresponsibly and has to **accept the consequences**. This is a perfect time to help him/her understand that he/she is still a good person and that next time he/she can choose to act in a more responsible manner.
3. **Assist** students to process what caused them to act irresponsibly so they can avoid acting that way in the future. They will learn to look at the situation as an **opportunity to learn** rather than a chance to berate themselves or feel negative about who they are.

CATCH THEM BEING RESPONSIBLE:

1. **Give students as many chances as needed.** Catch them when they do take responsibility and acknowledge them for how responsibly they have behaved.
2. An additional comment about how proud they must be of themselves is always helpful. It is fine for us to be proud of them and even better for them to **acknowledge themselves** when appropriate. The more times we can have students and children **internalize their behavior** the more esteemed they become.

Teachers can teach responsibility

When a student has been absent from class, they have an opportunity to take responsibility for finding out what work they missed. As the teacher you can set up a system that will allow them to do this. The students need to understand your expectation for them to take responsibility for finding out what work was missed. They need to be shown several ways they can accomplish this without asking the teacher. Perhaps the teacher could have a book, accessible to the students, in which he/she records all of the assignments and daily work, so they can easily retrieve the missed information.

Students could also have a phone buddy or two so when they are gone they can call their buddy and get the assignments either the day they return or the next day. When they do take responsibility for their missed work, ask them how they feel about acting so responsibly and tell them how helpful it was to you to have them do this.

There are dozens of ways that a student can be encouraged to take responsibility for his/her actions so that taking responsibility will become ingrained into the process of living. Getting students to access where and how they could have changed the outcome of an event by using a different thought and/or action process will allow students to experience what true responsibility is and how empowering and esteeming it is to be a responsible person. It is a gift to learn about consequences because they are always out there in the world. Let's start students out with as strong a foundation in responsibility as we hope to give them in the 3 R's or 7 R's. This is also another perfect tool for building internal locus of control.

Definitive Differences Between the Terms "Discipline" And "Punishment"

Punishment:

1. It is imposed. Done to someone. Responsibility is assumed by the punisher. It is external.
2. No belief in the student.
3. Open or concealed anger.
4. Easy or expedient.
5. A teaching process that usually reinforces failure identity. Essentially negative and short term without personal involvement.
6. Options for individual are closed.
7. Operates out of fear.
8. Produces dependency

9. Expresses power of a personal authority. Is usually painful and based on retribution or revenge (what happened in the past).
10. Based on telling.

Discipline:

1. Responsibility is assumed by the individual. Is desired. Is internal. Based on choices and consequences.
2. Strong belief in student.
3. Friendly.
4. Difficult and time consuming.
5. An active teaching process involving close, sustained, personal involvement. Emphasize teaching ways to act that will result in more successful behavior.
7. Operates out of love.
8. Promotes independence.
9. Based on logical or natural consequences expressing the reality of the social order (rules which must be learned in order to function adequately) Concerned with what will happen now, (the present).
10. Based on asking.

There are hundreds of opportunities for parents and teachers to allow and encourage students to take responsibility and to make responsible choices and decisions. It is imperative to give students the chance to practice this fine art and to learn to depend on themselves. One of the best ways to guide students to the path of taking responsibility is to teach them how to set goals and determine their own life direction. In the next chapter we will briefly discuss goal-setting.and its definite benefits to reaching goal achievement.

CHAPTER 7

GOAL SETTING:

"IF YOU DON'T KNOW WHERE YOU ARE GOING, YOU MIGHT END UP SOMEPLACE ELSE"

CHAPTER 7

GOAL SETTING: "If You Don't Know Where You Are Going, You Just Might Not Get There".

One of the ways to assist students in building self-esteem is to build-in incremental successes every day. It is important that students generate some **goals, both personal and academic,** so that they have something to be working toward that is of primary importance to them as individuals. Be sure that as the **teacher or parent** you **do not judge** the goals that students set for themselves. Your job is to **teach them how and why to set goals.** Remember, most students, and adults, do not set goals. They go passively through life waiting for life to happen to them because someone has always been there to tell them what is best for them. **Setting goals is taking an active role in your own life. It is an empowering and esteeming activity which teaches us that we are in charge.** Students must be taught that they are in charge of their own lives especially in **regards to classroom behavior and academic achievement.**

Setting Goals and Praising

We must teach each student to:

1. **Set goals that are attainable.**
   This is good practice at being realistic.

87

2. Make a <u>commitment</u> to attain the goal.
The **commitment** is what will keep the person working toward the goal, even if they get off track.

3. Praise yourself every day some action is taken toward attaining goal.

The way one can praise yourself consists of two parts:

o The first part describes the action for which you are praising

o The second part affirms that you are a good person, whether or not you have taken the action.

"I liked the way I resisted eating the candy I was offered so I would stay on my diet and reach my goal to be 12 pounds lighter by Christmas. I am a committed person."

4. Write the goal down where it can be seen daily. When you see it, reflect on what you have done to reach the goal.

Reminders and what to do when you get off track
When a person reflects on the progress toward her goal and notices that some of her actions are not helping her reach the goal, she could give herself a reminder. The reminder consists of an explanation of:

1. What action took you away from your goal
2. How you could rectify that action
3. Praising yourself for noticing you were temporarily off the goal path and for getting back on track toward your goal.
4. Acknowledging yourself for being such a conscientious person.

Explanations are not excuses. They are very different. **An excuse is used for protection. An explanation is used for knowledge and growth.**

When and How to Adjust Your Goals

As you reflect on your progress toward your goal, you will begin to realize whether or not your progress is satisfactory for you. If it is not satisfactory, you have two choices. You can choose to try other actions to move toward your goal or you can choose to adjust your goal.

For example, Ellis' goal as a boy was to become a professional basketball player. He spent hours practicing. He learned much about the game. As he got older he realized that he was not going to be tall enough to play in the pros. At this time he chose to accept this fact and he began to participate in other activities like tennis and softball. Eventually he developed new goals related to his new interests. This type of goal adjusting is important for everyone. Some of our students, however, tend to perceive this as failure and use the failure to put themselves down. This negative cycle tends to lower one's self-esteem. It is important for students to recognize when to adjust a goal and when to try other actions to reach that goal.

The key element in Ellis's story that he was not going to be tall enough-was very certain. In some cases the realization is not so clear and sometimes a student's poor perception of reality will cause him/her to adjust a goal unrealistically. Students need to be taught how to get outside help in diagnosing their situation when the goal is an important one.

The significant parts of this section are two-fold:

1. Students need to be taught the art of goal setting
2. Students must be clear that adjusting goals is natural and needed as growth and change occur

Adjusting Goals Is Never Equal To Failure

Each time we review a goal, we automatically evaluate where we are and how that fits with where we want to be. That is a perfect time for making changes in our lives. That gives us a sense of empowerment once again. Increased personal empowerment builds self-esteem. That "I can do anything I put my mind and **commitment** to " feeling, gives one an extraordinary sense of **self-respect, self-confidence, and self-esteem.**

CHAPTER 8

LEARNING/PERSONALITY STYLES:

AN AWARENESS TOOL TO ENHANCE SELF-ESTEEM BY KNOWING YOUR TRUE COLORS

CHAPTER 8

LEARNING/PERSONALITY STYLES:
An Awareness Tool To Enhance Self-Esteem

Teaching to a variety of learning styles will improve students' self-esteem as well as their academic performance. The basic learning styles are:

1. Auditory
2. Visual
3. Kinesthetic/Tactile

There are **three modalities** through which people learn: **auditory, visual, and kinesthetic/tactile.** Much has been studied and discovered about learning styles and how they influence possibilities of student academic success. Although there have been many people who have studied and researched this subject and acknowledged the important relationship to a successful academic experience, **still, many educators do not teach with a view toward "reaching" students through their learning/personality styles**, nor do most educators make children aware of their own styles of learning. There is a good chance that if educators did make them aware, students would then take responsibility, even at an early age, in assuring that they were getting information in a way that could enhance their learning and retention. If student awareness of learning styles were encouraged more frequently, students and teachers would become partners in the

91

learning process, and both would have a key to unlocking some of the mysteries of learning success.

The dominant mode of instruction in traditional classroom education is an **auditory** mode. Many teachers constantly talk at students giving lectures, instructions, directions, reprimands, etc. The fact is that a very small percent of the population learns by **auditory** instruction. The figure is somewhere between **8%** and **12%.** Although teachers occasionally throw in some visual stimulus such as writing on the chalkboard, films, video tapes, slides, and overheads, etc., only about **38%** of the population are **visual** learners. Approximately **10%** of all learners use **both auditory and visual** modalities interchangeably.

That leaves a huge number of students who are **kinesthetic** learners, (40%), unable to sit for long periods of time without tactile learning experiences to keep them engaged in the learning process. Yet only about **15%,** or less, of **instruction** is done in this modality. It should not surprise anyone that **the number of students who drop out of school, between 35-45%, correlates highly to the number of those who learn through the kinesthetic modality.** These are students who have particularly low self-esteem. If a student is engaged for only 15% of the time, and the rest of the time they aren't "getting the message", it is no wonder they claim to be "bored", "sick of school", "ignored", and "not able to sit still". They may look for distractions just to take themselves away from the learning process because that process does not work for them.

This is the population of students with whom teachers are impatient because those students don't seem interested in what is being taught. More often than not, if we would present a few kinesthetic activities to enhance the learning process, these students would have a better than even chance of producing. Evidence shows that students not only can understand the material, but are creative in their approaches when demonstrating that fact. Upon those occasions when a teacher has a class filled with kinesthetic learners, it becomes absolutely vital that the group have the majority of the lessons presented in a tactile modality. How is a teacher to know why a particular class may not be working well, if there is no knowledge of the student's learning styles? A creative change in the presentations of lessons by the teacher could make all the difference in how the class behaves and learns.

The following overview will give teachers a way to recognize and understand these learning types, and a way to begin to engage them more extensively in the learning process. This could improve the success ratio of individuals and among the entire class as well. **Nothing succeeds like success. It is a sure way to build high self-esteem among students.**

PERSONALITY/LEARNING STYLES
(TRUE COLORS)

Although the concepts of **TRUE COLORS** information in its entirety cannot possibly be presented here, it can be overviewed in bits and pieces, to some extent. It is important to include an awareness of **TRUE COLORS** in this book, so that teachers can be aware of its existence, and perhaps avail themselves of this new and powerful information. Having knowledge of TRUE COLORS will give a teacher more assistance in the teaching/learning process than almost any other tool

I have found in my twenty years of teaching. In-service trainings and workshops in TRUE COLORS have proven to boost test scores, teacher understanding of students, connectiveness between teacher and student, as well as between student and student. It has also assisted students and teachers to realize the differences in human beings and hence to become more tolerant of these differences.

TRUE COLORS, created by Don Lowry, is a method for individuals to determine for themselves their personality/learning style and why they and others behave the way they do under certain conditions. This method is tied in closely with Keirsy-Bates and Myers-Briggs learning style assessment tests. The primary difference is that the TRUE COLORS method is quick, simple, and can be a tool for "diagnosis" almost on the spot. People fall into four basic categories of colors: Gold, Blue, Green, and Orange

This diagnosis can assist teachers in developing a clearer understanding of why students behave the way they do and how to break the pattern of failure established by "at risk" students by providing assignments which esteem students and bring about success. A very brief overview of **TRUE COLORS,** a learning/personality styles test is very esteeming because it brings all students into the group of over-all successful learners. It also shows that each and every student has gifts and talents to share with the group and the world at large. It points out how valuable each "color" is and acknowledges the good in all human beings. The insight gained by those who engage in this simple exercise --putting **four cards** in order, according to how one sees oneself, is very helpful for both student and teacher. In addition, it is fun, enlightening, and useful as a tool for growth and understanding for both groups, as well as for parents.

According to Don Lowry, the creator of TRUE COLORS, "the TRUE COLORS person is a person of excellence who has a positive state of mind, who recognizes and acknowledges others' perspectives, and participates in their own unique way in improving the quality of life for every individual."

An overview of the "TRUE COLORS" characteristics will provide the bare minimum of how to begin to "evaluate" learning/personality styles:

GOLD: People can count on me - my actions can be predicted - I am always ready for tomorrow - I am loyal, giving, and like to take care of others - I am practical and sensible - I value home and family and have a strong sense of right and wrong I follow rules and respect authority.

GREEN: I am curious, investigating, and form my own ideas - I look at the big picture - I am cool, calm, an collected - I like to be smart - I enjoy activities that require problem-solving - I value intelligence, insight, fairness, and justice - I like to set my own standards and I enjoy seeking fundamental truths.

BLUE: I look for meaning in my life - I like to get along with people and look after them - I like to express myself - I am honest and like to be told I am doing well - I fit in well in most situations - I want to be important in people's lives - I think about the future, a perfect world, good friends, and love.

ORANGE: I like action! To go for it on a moment's notice - I am witty, charming, and bold - I see life as a game, here and now - I act on impulse - I like adventure - I like to compete, and I am skillful in what I do - I like fun, change, and excitement - I live life to the limit and have a cheerful outlook - I learn by doing and am a natural trouble-shooter.

Each "color" has good, positive characteristics. In addition, there is a direct correlation between the "colors" of the students and the modality in which they best learn. Teachers can acquire a handle on how to better serve their students, not only by teaching them in the proper modality, and by understanding their behavior patterns, but by esteeming them for who they are, and using tools to promote and encourage their participation in the learning process. Students have been known to go from D's and F's to B's and A's when both teachers and students are made aware of their learning styles through their primary and secondary colors. It is impossible to do justice to this very exciting method of analysis in such a short space. The primary purpose of the TRUE COLORS approach, is to help prevent school dropouts by building a better school climate, student self-esteem and professional growth information and a learning opportunity for teachers.

The four major groups, representing styles of behavior and some of the major "turn-ons" with information on how they gain their **esteem** are as follows:

1. The <u>GOLD</u> group (51% of the adult population) whose members **derive much of their self-esteem by being "responsible."** They value loyalty, dependability, conformity, punctuality, and order. A stable family and work life is essential to their esteem. In that connection, they use words such as "morals" and "good character".

2. The <u>BLUE</u> group (22% of the adult population) thinks of itself as **being "authentic".** Blues value honesty, sincerity, caring, and nurturing others. They gain satisfaction from harmony and unity. They speak easily of "self-esteem" and "feeling good about oneself".

3. The <u>GREEN</u> group (13% of the adult population) is characterized by being "curious" ingenious, creating new ideas and concepts, invention, designs, and models. They enjoy problem-solving and intellectual achievements. Their **self-esteem is described in terms of "dignity," "self-concept," "pride," and "efficacy".**

4. The <u>ORANGE</u> group (14% of the adult population) is more "adventurous." Esteem comes from spur-of-the-moment actions, doing things that require variation and flexibility. They are goal-oriented and like to pursue fun and excitement. "Self-confident" is their primary self-esteem description.

I began to gain interest in "TRUE COLORS" a number of years ago when I was doing research on dropouts and the characteristics they manifested. The one piece of information that boggled my mind about what "TRUE COLORS" revealed is that approximately fifty-five percent of the people who go in to education are Gold and approximately **forty percent of the students who drop out of school are Orange.** The Green part of my mind ran with that one and I was clear that this was a tool that I wanted to learn more about. I have been using it with great success, at the Independent Learning Center. Our school, which is designed as a dropout recovery school, strives to help students get in touch with what might have happened to them in the past and how they have the power to change those past occurences, now that they have a greater understanding about themselves.

Generally, overall style and orientation remain fairly constant throughout a person's life. There are some changes in relative orientation as people mature. The way the TRUE COLORS tool works is by having students and teachers "colorize" themselves which divides them into color categories. They select their primary and secondary colors, which leads to further information for both student and teacher. For example, teachers could tell which students they were not reaching as well as others, thereby varying the modality in which they present lessons to the particular "color" of student. They might also be more inclined to use a different assessment tool, such as portfolios for the "orange" student who is more kinesthetic than a "gold" student. One school in Monroe, North Carolina used TRUE COLORS to check student academic performance and reported numbers of failing grades according to color. They have learned some very interesting things and can address that issue differently than they have in the past. They are developing data to begin a study on curriculum, teaching and learning styles as well. This is only the beginning.

In the home, TRUE COLORS knowledge can affect relationships within the family group in a number of ways, i.e. resolving problems, improving understanding, improving communication with children and spouses, relief of stress, etc.

In business, TRUE COLORS can affect overall employee attendance, team building, task alignment, productivity, employee-management relations, staff meetings, etc.

In the community, TRUE COLORS can affect organizations and their effectiveness, church groups, law enforcement agencies, social service agencies and their effectiveness level, etc.

In schools, overall attendance of students and staff, effectiveness of counselors with students, parents, as well as the relationship between teachers, administrators, counselors and students, activities, and communication can be enhanced by the use of TRUE COLORS.

The first step with TRUE COLORS is to help students appreciate their own strengths and weaknesses and to recognize strengths and weaknesses in their classmates. Personality and learning styles can be the foundation to helping each student better understand each person's communication process. It helps students evaluate how individuals perceive and react to different stimuli. They learn that to be "different" is okay. That alone would be a great boost to students and their interest level even if it were all the program did. And it can do a whole lot more.

I really enjoy presenting TRUE COLORS to teachers because it provides valuable information about our students and ourselves. But more important to me is that its knowledge has helped to transform both teachers and students. It serves the curious, the harmonious, the responsible, and the adventurous. While we go about the business of restructuring, let's put a little fun and enjoyment in it, and move toward a whole new consciousness about each other. There is always more to learn about the important jobs we have as educators and parents. Any tool that helps us do that job better is appreciated. TRUE COLORS is fun and educationally valuable. It is one more tool to promote self-esteem, the necessary ingredient for success.

AFTERWORD

I realize that nothing in life is ever complete, including this book. Each time I sat down to edit what I had written, I added more material and when the end was upon me, I thought, "Oh, no. There is so much I have left out." For me that is a challenge for the next time.

There is much more to learn about self-esteem and many ways to learn it. The California Council to Promote Self-Esteem and Responsibility, an organization which I currently Chair, is designed to network the fifty-eight counties throughout California, in order to share new ideas, research, information, conferences, exemplary programs and people who may serve to bring California, and any other states with similar interests, TOWARD A STATE OF ESTEEM. The organization has a wonderful newsletter, filled with pertinent information on self-esteem, which we mail throughout the country. Our editor is Tom Rische, a retired teacher and gifted writer, from Los Angeles, who also serves on the Los Angeles Self-Esteem Task Force. Copies of our Mission Statement, Vision Statement, and Goals, are available upon request at the address on the copyright page of this book if you are interested in being on the mailing list or becoming a member.

There are a great many schools and programs and curriculums which are begining to address the issue of self-esteem in very positive ways.

One such school, Mirage Elementary School, is located in the Deer Valley Unified School District in Glendale, Arizona. At Mirage a strong emphasis is placed on a safe learning environment. Students and staff are encouraged to maintain a positive attitude and foster productive interpersonal relationships. For several years the Sixth Grade students have participated in the Phoenix Police Department's D.A.R.E. program to promote self-esteem, develop refusal skills, and become role models for younger students. An additional program was implemented for Fourth Graders to supplement the D.A.R.E. program and to reach students of a younger age.

Through the guidance of the Scottsdale Prevention Institute, classroom teachers were trained to use the structure of the <u>Skills Streaming Program</u> (by McGinnis and Goldstein-Research Press Co., Champaign, IL) in their homerooms. Students participate in class meetings to solve current problems and learn self-management in several areas.

Students have the opportunity for self-expression in a writing program that spans an integrated curriculum. Every month has a theme that promotes cooperation and success and each morning the principal announces a positive thought for the day. Many teachers encourage students to write the thought in their journals tin the form of an affirmation. Students also have the opportunity to read their writing to Trish Dolasinsky, the school principal, during the scheduled times of the Principal's Writing Program. Mrs. Dolasinsky has supported teachers' efforts to maintain orderly learning by providing needed counseling and positive phone calls home for deserving students.

The staff's efforts have changed a campus with an often chaotic, inconsistent structure to one of cooperation, enjoyment and mutual respect. It is not uncommon to hear students repeat to other students on of the more popular affirmations, "We want everyone at Mirage to be successful."

Another wonderful curriculum used as a one semester individualized or group curriculum which covers, in detail with explanations and exercises which support every aspect of what I have been discussing was written by Vicki Phillips, a Continuation High School Principal for use with her own students. The curriculum is called **Personal Development** and is designed to promote self-esteem, communication skills, goal-setting, problem solving, and create a sense of responsibility in at-risk high school students. I know that the exercises can be easily used at the Junior High level also. If there is any interest, I will be happy to give you prices and an overview of the curriculum. It is one of the best I have seen. In fact I am now using it in my own school.

There are dozens of other programs that are exemplary and effective now being implemented across the United States. Thank goodness. I am anxious to hear from colleagues who have such a program to share. I plan to highlight the human side of these success stories in my next book. Please write and let me know about what is working for students.

According to June Edwards (author of "To Teach Responsibility, Bring Back the Dalton Plan", an article in the January, 1991, issue of Phi Delta Kappan magazine), "Today's schools are designed as though students will face the same kind of life as their grandparents. In previous generations, children were trained for industrial work. They learned to be punctual, obedient to authority, and tolerant of repetition, boredom and discomfort, for such was the lot of factory workers. Judgement, decision-making ability, creativity, and independence were neither taught nor desired."

Industries have changed in recent years and schools must follow. Although many "...classrooms are teacher-centered, focused on isolated facts, and constrained by standardized curricula and tests,..." there is a change beginning. As teachers, we must accept responsibility for factors we can control. We can create a safe and esteeming environment in our classrooms. We can help students learn to be responsible, to make decisions, to work together, to be creative, to communicate effectively, to take academic risks, and most of all, to value each other as human beings.

As Edwards says, **"Teachers must give up their center stage role and become guides, facilitators, and friends."**

By adopting an attitude that our students are responsible and capable and caring, we can facilitate their development into adults who have high self-esteem and positive regard for others and for our society. I am convinced that teachers and parents can do this. We are the agents for change, and the hope of the future is in our hands. **Together we can make a difference.**

I want to leave you with my favorite story, in case you have not yet acknowledged how important you are and how much of a difference you really make in the world.

A man is walking along the beach in Mexico and he notices a person further down the beach, kneeling down, picking something up, and throwing it into the water. As he walks closer he sees the person repeat the same actions, kneeling down, picking something up and throwing it into the water. Finally he gets up to the person and asks,
"What are you doing?"
The person says, "These are starfish and when they wash up on the shore, they die. So I am throwing them back into the water."
The man said, "That's ridiculous. There are hundreds of beaches in the world with thousands of starfish that wash up on the shores. Throwing them back into the water, what difference does it make?"
*The person bent down, picked up a starfish, threw it back into the water and said, "It made a difference to **that one.**"*

I leave you for now knowing how much of a difference you make to every person with whom you come in contact, both adult and child, and especially the children..

Through esteeming yourself, you esteem others.
Through esteeming others, you esteem yourself.
Self-Esteem is the necessary ingredient for success.

REFERENCES

Blanchard, Ken, Inner Management Tapes, Blanchard Training & Development, Inc., 125 State Place, Escondido, CA 92025-9878

California Task Force to Promote Self-Esteem and Personal and Social Responsibility, Toward a State of Esteem, Bureau of Publications, California State Department of Education, P. O. Box 271, Sacramento, CA 95802-2721; 916-445-1260

Carlton, Nancy, At-Risk Youth Demonstration Program Deputy Director, Yolo County Community Partnership Agency, 112 West Main Street, Woodland, CA 95695, 916-661-2900

Clemes, Harris, Ph.D. and Bean, Reynold, Ed.M., How to Raise Children's Self-Esteem, Price Stern Sloan Publishers, Inc., 410 North Cienega Blvd, Los Angeles, CA 90048

Collins, Cindy, Problems of Teenagers Today (List), 1539 N. China Lake Blvd., #624, Ridegecrest, CA 93555; 619-371-6773

Community Board Program, Inc., The, Conflict Resolution: A Secondary Curriculum, 149 Ninth Street, San Francisco, CA 94103; 415-552-1250

Edwards, June, To Reach Responsibility, Bring Back the Dalton Plan, Phi Delta Kappan, January, 1991, Phi Delta Kappa, Inc., P.O. Box 789, Bloomington, IN 47402

Gordon, Dr. Thomas, Teacher Effectiveness Training, Effectiveness Training, Inc., 531 Stevens Avenue, Solana Beach, CA 92075-2093; 619-481-8121

Green, Brad, Self-esteem: A Manual for Helping Others, Consultant in Quality Schools Program , 938 Rivera Street, Simi Valley, CA 93065; 805-527-5291

Hipp, Earl, Fighting Invisible Tigers, Free Spirit Publishing, 400 First Avenue North, Suite 616, Minneapolis, MN 55401; 612-338-2068

Kaufman, Gershen, Ph.D. and Raphael, Lev, Ph.D., Stick Up for Yourself, Free Spirit Publishing, 400 First Avenue North, Suite 616, Minneapolis, MN 55401; 612-338-2068

Korbel, Jim, Branches,.Training and Educational Director, United Farm Workers, AFL-CIO,

LaMeres, Clare, The Winner's Circle Yes, I Can, La Meres Lifestyles Unlimited, P.O. Box 8326, Newport Beach, CA 92658

Lowry, Don, True Colors, Communication Companies International, 291 Boat Canyon Drive, Laguna Beach, CA 92651

Marston, Stephanie, The Magic of Encouragement, Raising Miracles-Educational Seminars, 870 Galloway Street, Pacific Palisades, CA 90272; 213-459-8775

Redenbach, Sandi, <u>Self-Awareness Program,</u>
<u>A Component of the California Teachers Association</u>
<u>High Risk Training Program, Trainer's Manual and</u>
<u>Participant's Handbook</u> ,Esteem Seminar Programs,
313 Del Oro Ave., Davis, CA 95616 916-756-8678
or 916-666-0264

Stanford, Gene, Ph.D., <u>Self-Esteem - Globe Health</u>
<u>Program,</u> Globe Book Company, Inc., 50 West 23rd
Street, New York, NY 10010

BIBLIOGRAPHY

100 Ways to Enhance Self-Concept in the Classroom by Jack Canfield and Harold C. Wells, of Self-Esteem Seminars, 17156 Palisades Cr., Pacific Palisades, CA 90272

Belonging by Jane Devencinzi and Susan Pendergast, BELONGING, 2960 Hawk Hill Lane, San Luis Obispo, CA 93401; 805-543-7131

Circles of Learning: Cooperation in the Classroom by David Johnson, Roger Johnson, Patricia Roy, and Edythe Holubec, California ASCD, P. O. Box 1239, Upland, CA   91786

Cooperative Discipline by Linda Albert, American Guidance Service, Publisher Building, P. O. Box 99, Circle Pines, Minnesota 55014-9989; 1-800-328-2560

Developing Self-Esteem by Connie Palladino, Ph.D., Crisp Publications, Inc., 95 First Street, Los Altos, CA 94022; 415-949-4888

Difference Makers by Helice Bridges of Different Makers, Inc., P. O. Box 2115, Del Mar, CA 92014; 619-943-7490

Discipline with Dignity by Richard Curwin and Allen Mendler, California ASCD, P.O. Box 1239, Upland, CA 91786

He Hit Me Back First by Eva D. Fugitt, Jalmar Press, 45 Hitching Post Drive, Building 2, Rolling Hills Estates, CA 90274, Eva Fugitt Associates, 1100 Vista Drive, Fortuna, CA 95540; 707-725-2224

How to Raise Children's Self-Esteem, How to Raise Teenagers' Self-Esteem, How to Discipline Children Without Feeling Guilty, How to Teach Children Responsibility by Harris Clemes, Ph.D. and Reynold Bean, Ed.M., Price Stern Sloan Publishers, Inc., 410 North Cienega Blvd., Los Angeles, CA 90048

Self-Esteem: Awareness Program, A Component of the California Teachers Association High-Risk Training Program by Sandi Redenbach, Esteem Seminar Programs, 313 Del Oro Avenue, Davis, CA 95616; 916-756-8678 or 916-666-0264.

The One Minute Manager by Kenneth Blanchard and Spencer Johnson, Blanchard Training and Development, Inc., 125 State Place Escondido, CA 92025-9878

The Social Importance of Self-Esteem edited by Andrew M. Mecca, Neil J. Smelser, and John Vasconcellos, University of California Press, Berkeley, CA 94720

The Winning Family Increasing Self-Esteem In Your Children and Yourself by Louise Hart, LifeSkills Press, P.O. Box 9276, Oakland, CA 94613

True Colors by Don Lowry, Communication Companies International, 291 Boat Canyon Drive, Laguna Beach, CA 92651

BIBLIOGRAPHY OF RESEARCH

Support for the Significance of Self-Esteem

Beane, James, and Lipka, Richard; Self-Concept, Self-Esteem and the Curriculum, New York, Teachers College Press, 1984.

Bledsoe, J., "Self-Concept of Children and their Intelligence, Achievement, Interests, and Anxiety", Child Educ 43: 436-38, 1967.

Block, D.A., "The Delinquent Integration", Psychiatry 15: 297-303, 1952.

Bloom, B.S.; "Affective Outcomes of School Learning", Phi Delta Kappa, 1977, pps. 193-199.

Branden, Nathaniel. Psychology of Self-Esteem, Los Angeles, CA; Bantam Books, Nash Publishing Company, 1969.

Brookover, W.B.; Self-Concept of Ability and School Achievement, East Lansing, Michigan; Office of Research and Public Information, Michigan State University, 1965.

Brunkan, R.J., and Sheni F., "Personality Characteristics of Ineffective, Effective and Efficient Readers", Personnel and Guid. J., 44: 837-44, 1966.

Combs, A.; "Affective Education or None at All," Educational Leadership, April, 1982.

Coopersmith, Stanley; The Antecedents of Self-
Esteem, San Francisco, CA; W.H. Freeman,
1967.

Covington, M.; "Self-Esteem and Failure in School,"
The Social Importance of Self-Esteem, U.C.
Press, Berkeley, CA.,1989.

Crockenberg, Susan and Soby, Barbara; "Self-
Esteem and Teenage Pregnancy,"
U.C. Press, Berkeley, CA 1989.

Earle, Janice: Female Dropouts: A New Perspective,
Alexandria, VA; National Association of State
Board of Education, 1987.

Fuellgrabe, U.; "Psychological Analysis of
Vandalism," Polizei-Feuhrungsakademie,
West Germany, 1980.

Gossop, M.; "Drug Dependence and Self-Esteem,"
International Journal of Addictions, Vol. II,
1976.

Holly, William; "Self-Esteem: Doesnt It Contribute to
Students Academic Success?" Eugene:
Oregon School Study Council, University of
Oregon, 1987.

Johnston, P.S.; "School Failure, School Attitudes and
the Self-Concept in Delinguest." ERIC
Document ED 173-712, 1977.

Kaplan, H.B.; Self-Attitudes and Deviant Behavior,
Goodyear, Pacific Palisades, CA 1975.

Keegan, Andrew; "Positive Self-Image - - A
    Cornerstone of Success," Guidepost,
    February 19, 1987.

Kelley, T.M.; "Changes in Self-Esteem Among Pre-
    Delinquent Youths in Voluntary Counseling
    Relationships," Juvenile and Family Court
    Journal, Vol. 29, May, 1978.

Kite, Hayman; How to Prevent Dropouts, Orlando
    Florida, 1989.

Kirst, Michael; Conditions of Children in California,
    Policy Analysis for California Education
    (PACE), U.C. Berkeley, 1990.

Reasoner, R. and Gilbert, R; Building Self-Esteem:
    Implementation Project Summary. ERIC
    Clearinghouse of Counseling and Personnel
    Services, "CG 02089", 1988.

Scheirer, M.A. and Kraut, R.; "Increasing Educational
    Achievement via Self-Concept Change,"
    Review of Education Research, Winter, 1979.

Skager, Rodney; Prevention of Drug and Alcohol
    Abuse. Sacramento California, California
    Attorney General's Office, 1988.

Steffenhagen, R.A. and Burns, Jeff D.; The Social
    Dynamics of Self-Esteem, New York, NY,
    Praeger, 1987.

Wilson, John; "Motivation, Modeling and Altruism,"
    Journal of Personality and Social Psychology,
    Vol. 34, December 1976.

ABOUT THE AUTHOR

Sandi Redenbach, a native of Boston, Massachusetts, who now resides in Davis, CA, is a graduate of the University of California, Davis. Her education career spans twenty years of classroom teaching. In addition to high school drama, speech, and English, she teaches classes in self-esteem, parenting, and rhetoric at several community colleges, adult education centers, and the University of California, Davis. She is the founder and coordinator of the Independent Learning Center, a drop-out recovery, independent study, high school in the Woodland Joint Unified School District, Woodland, CA.

She is an active member of her local, and state teachers associations and has carried several peices of legislation through the California State Assembly. Currently she is President of her county Phi Delta Kappa chapter. She is active in several alternative education organizations and is involved in Effective Schools and Restructuring movements.

A Mentor Teacher in multi-cultural education, and a California Teachers Association High Risk Cadre Trainer and self-esteem module writer, she is also a founder and current Chairperson of the California Council to Promote Self-Esteem and Responsibility.

Sandi has presented countless workshops throughout the United States. As President of her own consulting firm, Esteem Seminar Programs, her workshops, designed for teachers, students, parents, business professionals, and others interested in self-esteem, cover such topics as the importance of self-esteem, the conditions which allow it to develop, and the techniques for improving it.

She also presents workshops in Conflict Resolution, Team Building, Stress Reduction, and Personality and Learning Styles. Ms. Redenbach has received a number of awards for her work in Human Rights, as well as an outstanding educator award. She is an avid theatre buff, former actress and singer and a loyal Boston Red Sox and Boston Celtics fan.

Sandi, a former high school drop-out and "late bloomer" has made students' and teachers' well-being the focal point of her professional life. She believes that now is the time for America to realize the importance and power of education and educators and to make them our top national priority.

Your greatest contribution to humankind is to be sure that there is a teacher in every classroom, who cares that every student every day learns and grows and feels like a real <u>human</u> being.

This author is available for workshops, seminars, keynote addresses, in-service trainings, and consulting with schools, leadership teams, teachers, administrators, parent groups, law enforcement personnel, businesses and social service agencies.

<u>Sample of workshop titles are:</u>
-"At Risk" Youth: America's Time Bomb
-Building Self-Esteem: The Pathway to Academic
          Achievement
-Personality/Learning Styles: Knowing Your TRUE COLORS
-Educating for a Dynamic Multi-Cultural Society
-Role Playing for Conflict Resolution
-Restructuring America's Schools: A Community
          Responsibility
-Team Building: The First Step to Personal Empowerment
-Building Responsible Children: A Process of Esteem
          Building
-Building Self-Esteem for Healthy Family Relationships
-Promoting Loyalty and Raising Productivity in the
          Business Arena: A Process of Esteem

Workshops designed to empower individuals and promote self-esteem for lifelong success in personal and professional interactions.

For further information
Esteem Seminar Programs/Publications
Sandi Redenbach, President
313 Del Oro Ave.
Davis, CA 95616
(916) 756-8678

Esteem Seminar Programs and Publishing
Phone: (916) 756-8678 or (916) 666-0264

Please send the following:
<u>Self-Esteem: The Necessary</u>
<u>Ingredient for Success</u>
by Sandi Redenbach   **quantity**   **total**

    $10.00 each   _____   _____

California Residents add 7.25% sales tax   _____
Shipping and Handling: $2.00 for 1st item
& $.50 for each item after that   **shipping**   _____

                  Total   _____

Please send a Check or Money Order payable to:
Esteem Seminar Programs and Publishing
313 Del Oro Ave.
Davis, CA 95616

_____Check here to be on our mailing list.

_____Check here for **information on workshops.**

Audio/Video Tapes available
upon request
Ship to **(please print):**

_____

Address   _____

Phone   (___)_____

City_____State_____Zip_____